WORLD BOOK'S

YOUNG SCIENTIST

WORLD BOOK'S

YOUNG SCIENTIST

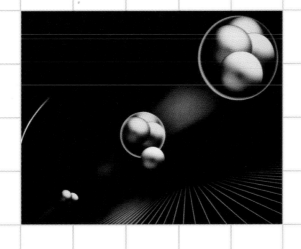

- ATOMS AND MOLECULES
- GASES

5

World Book, Inc.
a Scott Fetzer company
Chicago

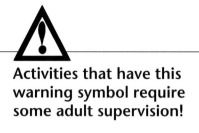

Activities that have this warning symbol require some adult supervision!

The quest to explore the known world and to describe its creation and subsequent development is nearly as old as mankind. In the Western world, the best-known creation story comes from the book of Genesis. It tells how God created Earth and all living things. Modern religious thinkers interpret the Biblical story of creation in various ways. Some believe that creation occurred exactly as Genesis describes it. Others think that God's method of creation is revealed through scientific investigation. *Young Scientist* presents an exciting picture of what scientists have learned about life and the universe.

World Book, Inc.
233 N. Michigan Avenue
Chicago, IL 60601

For information on other World Book products, call 1-800-WORLDBK (967-5325), or visit us at our Web site at http://www.worldbook.com

© 1997, 1995, 1991, 1990 World Book, Inc.

ISBN: 0-7166-2755-8 (volume V)
ISBN: 0-7166-2797-3 (set)

Library of Congress Catalog Card No. 00-107193

Printed in the United States of America

1 2 3 4 5 6 7 06 05 04 03 02 01 00

Contents

Atoms and molecules

Gases

ATOMS AND MOLECULES

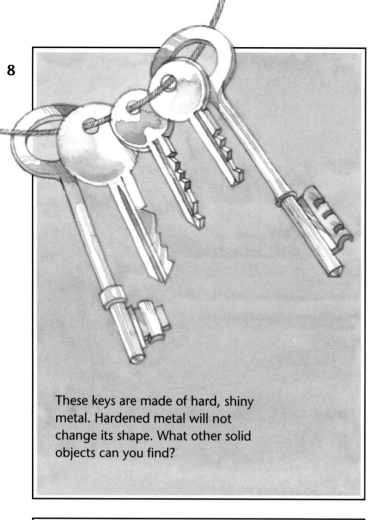

These keys are made of hard, shiny metal. Hardened metal will not change its shape. What other solid objects can you find?

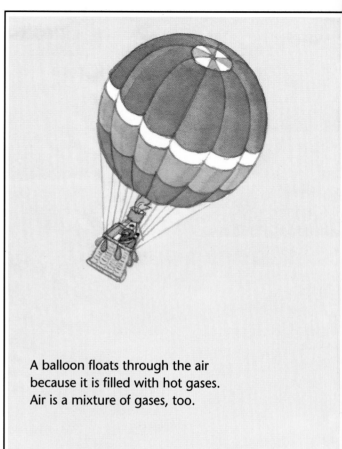

A balloon floats through the air because it is filled with hot gases. Air is a mixture of gases, too.

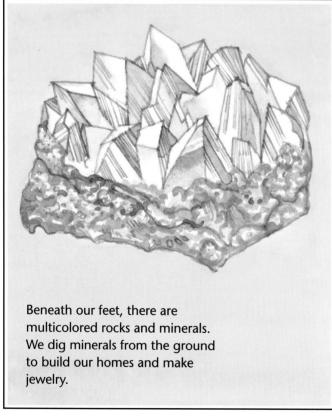

Beneath our feet, there are multicolored rocks and minerals. We dig minerals from the ground to build our homes and make jewelry.

We share Earth with many animals. This dazzling butterfly darts from flower to flower, gathering food.

You can pour a soft drink into a glass. But if you spill any, the liquid drink will spread out in a wet puddle.

The sunflower spreads its leaves and lifts its petals toward the sun. Earth is crowded with many different flowers, trees, and grasses.

What is the world made of?

The world is made up of all sorts of things. Just look around you. There are houses, cars, trees, and people. All these things are different shapes, sizes, and colors. Look closely at some of them. They are made from different materials. Some are hard and cold. Others are soft and warm. They may be wet or dry, rough or smooth. All these things look and feel different to us.

The different things in the world have two things in common. They are all made of something, which means they have **substance**, and they all take up space. Anything that takes up space and has weight is called **matter.** So a pencil, a book, a house, a tree, the air, and everything around you is matter. You are matter, too. Earth is all matter, and so are the stars throughout the universe and the dust that drifts between them.

What is matter?

Imagine you could divide a drop of water or a grain of sand. Then imagine you could divide them again and again, until the pieces are so small that you can no longer see them. Scientists can divide these tiny particles of matter even smaller under a powerful microscope. They divide them again and again, until the particles are so small that they can no longer be seen clearly, even under the microscope. Whatever in the end makes up matter is so small that we cannot see it. But everything in the world—animals, vegetables, minerals, solids, liquids, and gases—is made of matter.

Space and energy

Because space has no substance and obviously does not take up space, it does not qualify as matter. Neither does **energy**, which is the ability to do work.

However, matter and energy are not completely separate. Most scientists believe that matter and energy are two aspects of the same thing, like liquid water and ice are two aspects of water.

All these things are made of matter.

The building blocks of matter

Have you ever played with building blocks? The blocks can be joined together to make all kinds of things. Scientists think this is how the world is made up. Tiny particles join together, like building blocks, to make up matter. The matter in the universe is made from tiny particles called **atoms.** Millions and millions of atoms combine to make the different things around us—even the air we breathe. Atoms are the building blocks of matter.

Atoms are so small that they can't be seen. But scientists can take photographs of atoms using electron microscopes. With the help of these photographs, scientists can describe what atoms are like and build models to show how they behave.

Imagine that an atom is like a tiny solar system. In the center of the atom, there is a part called the **nucleus.** The nucleus contains particles called **protons** and **neutrons.** Whirling around the nucleus are much smaller, lighter particles called **electrons**, always in motion. You can think of the nucleus as the sun, and the electrons as Earth and other planets circling around the sun. There is constant motion in matter.

Electrons circle around the nucleus of an atom. A normal atom always has the same number of electrons as protons.

Protons and neutrons cluster together to make the nucleus of an atom.

Electrons, protons, and neutrons do not really look like balls. We draw them as balls to help us imagine how an atom behaves.

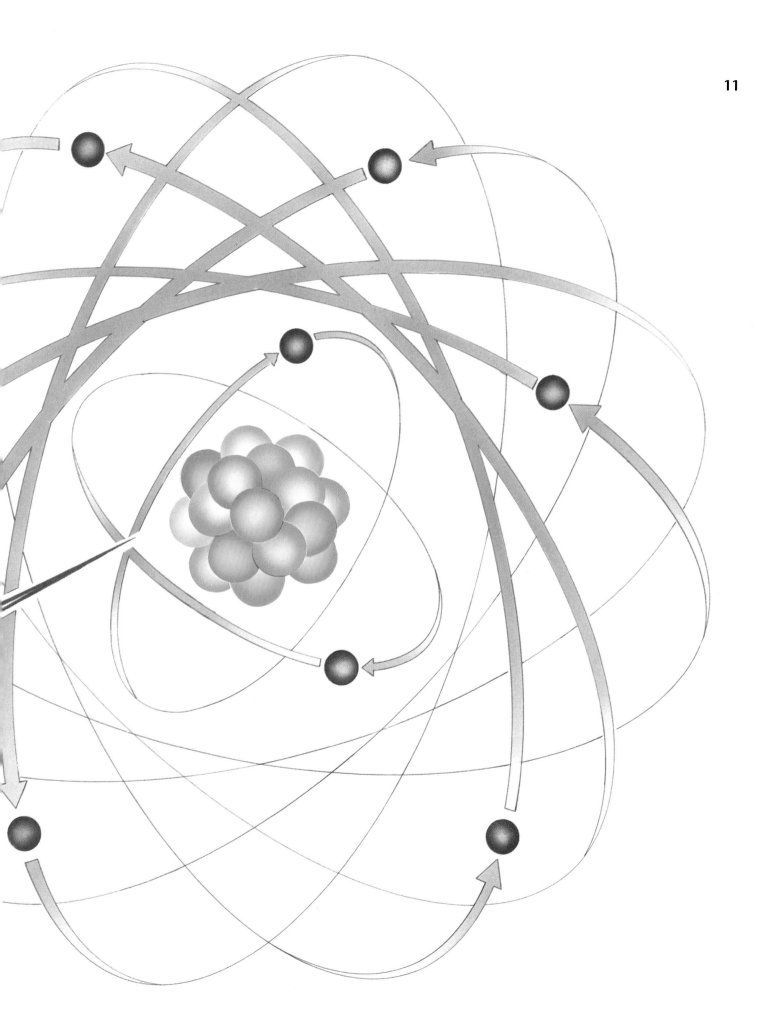

A collection of atoms

Matter around us is made up of atoms. But there is more than one type of atom. In fact, there are over one hundred different types, which make up the **elements.**

Elements are substances which are made up of many of the same type of atom. The metal called iron is an element made up of iron atoms. The gas called hydrogen is an element normally made up of pairs of hydrogen atoms. Elements are the simplest chemical substances. We don't often deal with atoms. Rather, we deal with the elements.

How can we tell an atom of iron from an atom of hydrogen? Each atom is made up of electrons circling around a nucleus. The nucleus is made up of protons and neutrons. A typical atom of hydrogen has only one proton and one electron. A typical atom of iron has 26 protons and 26 electrons. The number of neutrons can vary. But hydrogen will always have one proton and one electron, and iron will have 26 protons and 26 electrons. The number of protons determines the element.

These are drawings of the atoms of seven elements. Of these atoms, the hydrogen is the lightest and iron is the heaviest.

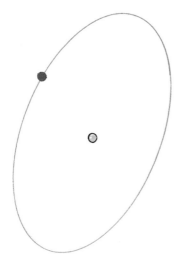

This atom of the element hydrogen has one proton, one electron, and no neutrons.

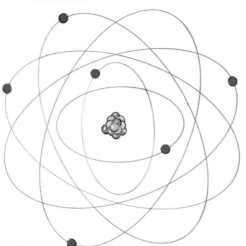

This atom of the element carbon has 6 protons, 6 neutrons, and 6 electrons.

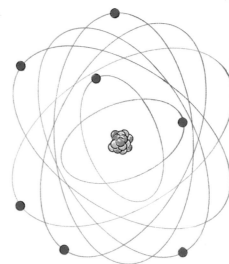

This atom of the element nitrogen has 7 protons, 7 neutrons, and 7 electrons.

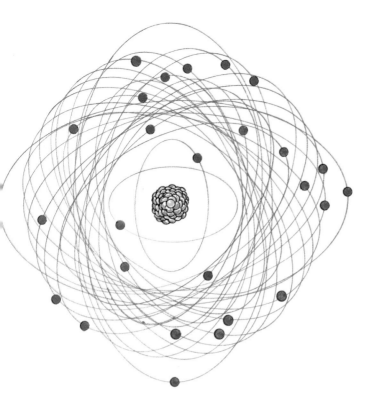

This atom of the element iron has 26 protons, 30 neutrons, and 26 electrons.

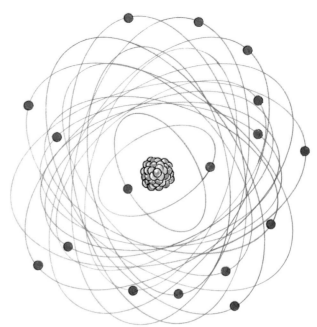

This atom of the element chlorine has 17 protons, 18 neutrons, and 17 electrons.

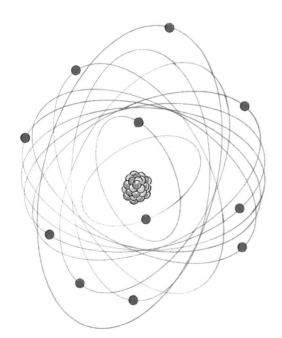

This atom of the element sodium has 11 protons, 12 neutrons, and 11 electrons.

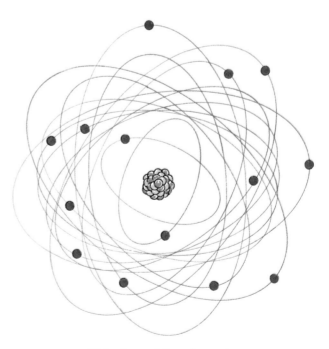

This atom of the element silicon has 14 protons, 14 neutrons, and 14 electrons.

Sorting the elements

Elements are the simplest recognized substances and together make up every other substance in the world. Scientists have found 109 different elements and may have created several more. With so many chemicals to work with, scientists often sort these elements into two groups—**metals** and **nonmetals**. Most elements are metals. Scientists have arranged the elements in a chart called the **periodic table of the elements**.

Look around your home. How many different metals can you find? The most common metals are aluminum and iron. You may also find some copper or gold. Other metals, such as brass, steel, and bronze, are made up of more than one metal.

You will need:

some iron nails

some nickel coins

a piece of charcoal

a steel spoon

some plastic-coated, copper wire

a 1.5-volt (D) battery

a 1.5-volt bulb
in a bulb holder

tape

Sorting metals from nonmetals

Here is a test that you can do to see how well an electric current passes through different elements.

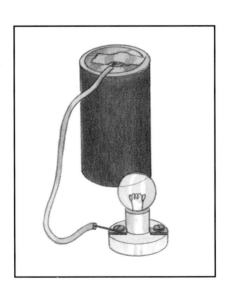

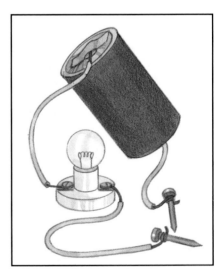

1. Cut three pieces of wire about 6 inches (15 centimeters) long. Attach the end of one piece to the battery. Fix the other end to the bulb.

2. Attach another piece of wire to the other side of the battery. Fix the third piece of wire to the other side of the bulb. Wind the two free ends of the wire around two iron nails.

Don't use a high-power battery—it will make the wires very hot.

Testing for metal

You can sort metal elements from nonmetal elements by testing them. Substances are tested by bending them, passing heat through them, and passing electricity through them. Some elements are solid but will bend and conduct heat easily. Electricity will also pass easily through these elements. They are **conductors** of electricity. The abilities to bend, to pass heat, and to conduct electricity are the **properties** of a metal. Elements such as iron, nickel, and copper are metals. Most of the elements are metals. Any element which does not share all the properties of a metal is called a nonmetal.

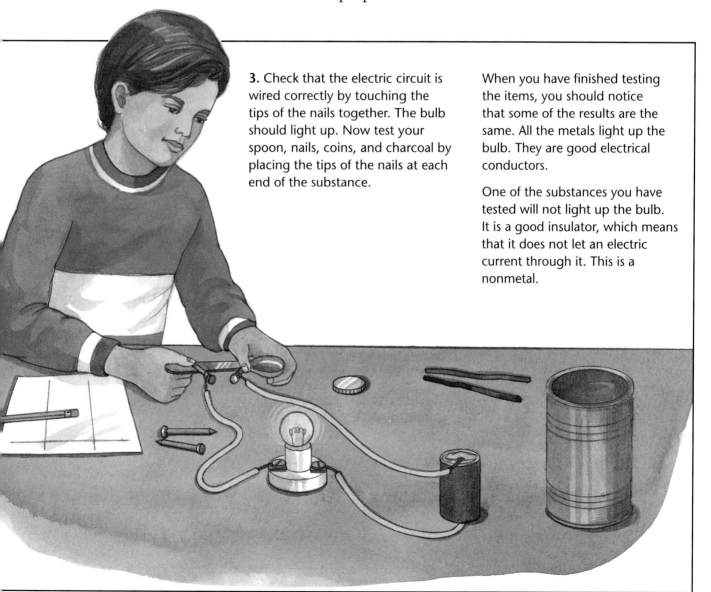

3. Check that the electric circuit is wired correctly by touching the tips of the nails together. The bulb should light up. Now test your spoon, nails, coins, and charcoal by placing the tips of the nails at each end of the substance.

When you have finished testing the items, you should notice that some of the results are the same. All the metals light up the bulb. They are good electrical conductors.

One of the substances you have tested will not light up the bulb. It is a good insulator, which means that it does not let an electric current through it. This is a nonmetal.

Joining atoms

Put a drop of water on a plate. See if you can cut it in half with a knife. Then try to divide each half in two. If it were somehow possible to go on making smaller parts of a drop of water, you would eventually reach the smallest part of water, a **molecule**. And splitting a molecule of water would result in two atoms of the element hydrogen and one atom of the element oxygen. The atoms join together to make a water molecule.

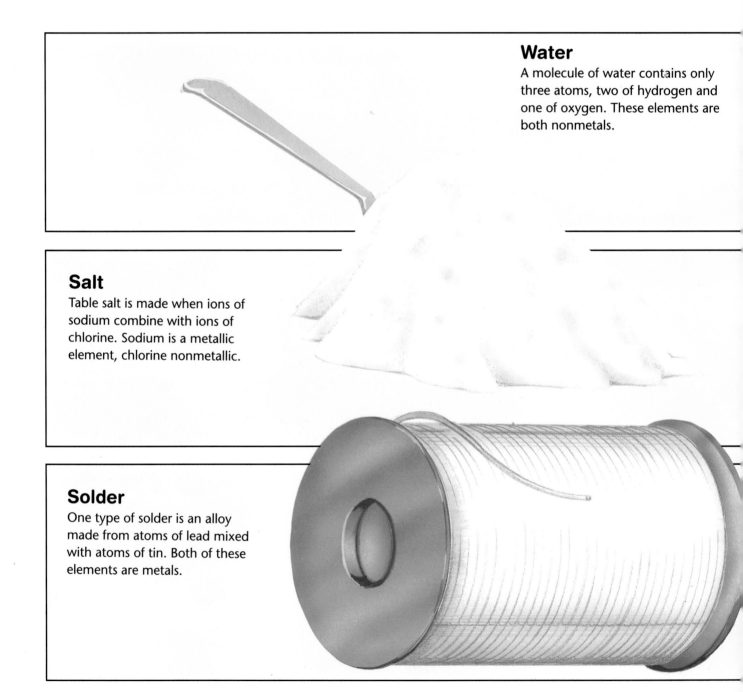

Water
A molecule of water contains only three atoms, two of hydrogen and one of oxygen. These elements are both nonmetals.

Salt
Table salt is made when ions of sodium combine with ions of chlorine. Sodium is a metallic element, chlorine nonmetallic.

Solder
One type of solder is an alloy made from atoms of lead mixed with atoms of tin. Both of these elements are metals.

Ions and alloys

Atoms of different elements don't always join together. But their ions might. If an atom were to lose or gain an electron, it would become an **ion**, an electrically charged atom. Ions can join together to form new substances that are held together by the electric charge. Atoms can mix together without forming ions. For example, an **alloy** is formed when atoms of two metal elements, or of a metal and another material, mix together.

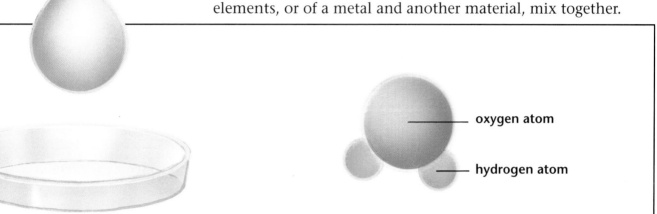

oxygen atom

hydrogen atom

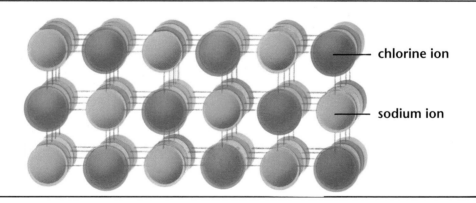

chlorine ion

sodium ion

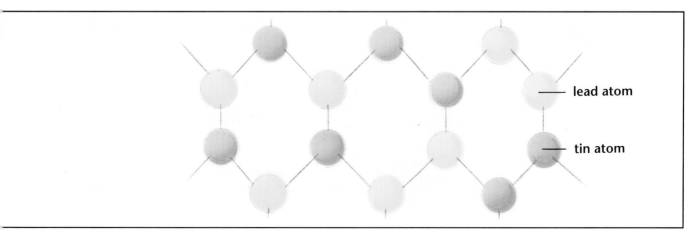

lead atom

tin atom

Salty water

If you stir a spoonful of ordinary salt crystals into some water, the crystals seem slowly to disappear. The salt has dissolved in the water. When something is dissolved in a liquid, the result is called a **solution.**

The substance that dissolves is called the **solute,** and the liquid that does the dissolving is called the **solvent.** Liquid water is a very good solvent. Try stirring half a teaspoonful of different solids into a glass of water. You will soon find out which substances are **soluble,** and will dissolve, and which are **insoluble,** or cannot dissolve.

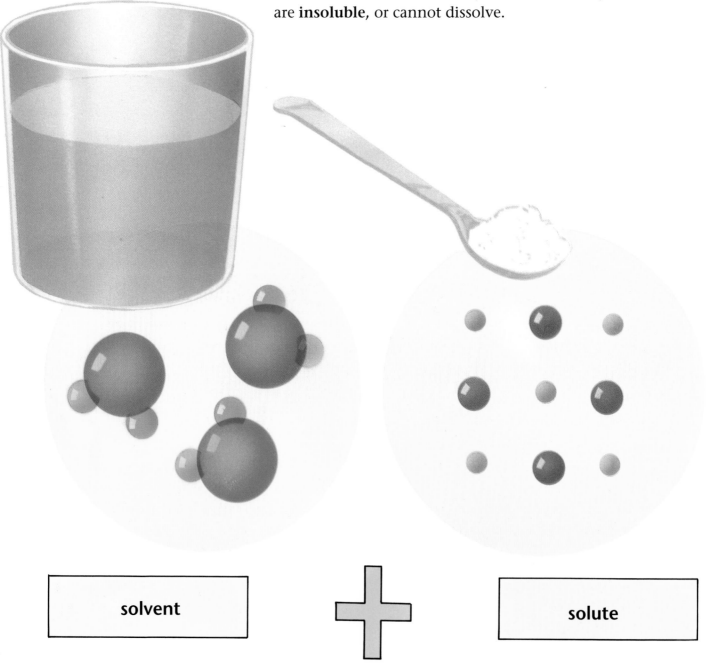

| solvent | + | solute |

Why does salt dissolve?

What happens to solids like salt crystals when they dissolve? The particles in a solid are fixed firmly together, but the particles in a liquid are free to move around. When salt mixes with water, the ions of sodium and chlorine attract the water molecules. The molecules surround the ions and separate them from each other. As more and more ions break free from the solid salt, it gradually seems to disappear.

If you put a lot of salt into a little water, there will not be enough water molecules to dissolve the salt ions. You need more water to dissolve the salt completely. Some solid substances will not dissolve. The water molecules can't separate the solid's atoms or ions from each other.

In a salt solution, the ions of sodium and chlorine are separated and surrounded by molecules of water, as shown below.

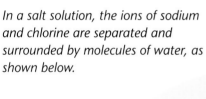

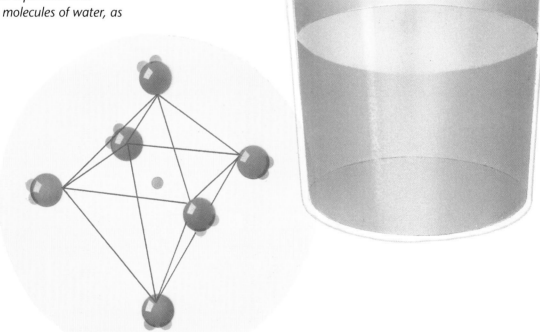

solution

Mixing and stirring

Elements are not usually found on their own. Most of them are in **mixtures** or **compounds**. Mixtures and compounds can be solids, liquids, or gases, and they are made up of atoms of more than one element.

Compounds

Salt is a compound of two elements called chlorine and sodium. The atoms of each element combine, or react together, to give a new substance. Sodium is a soft, metallic element that is so explosive it can be kept safely only in an airtight, moisture-free container or under a layer of oil. Chlorine is a poisonous yellow-green gas. These elements join together to make a compound called **sodium chloride**, or salt. This joining together is called a **chemical reaction**. Once they have reacted together, the atoms in the compound do not easily separate.

Sodium reacts with chlorine to give the compound sodium chloride, or salt.

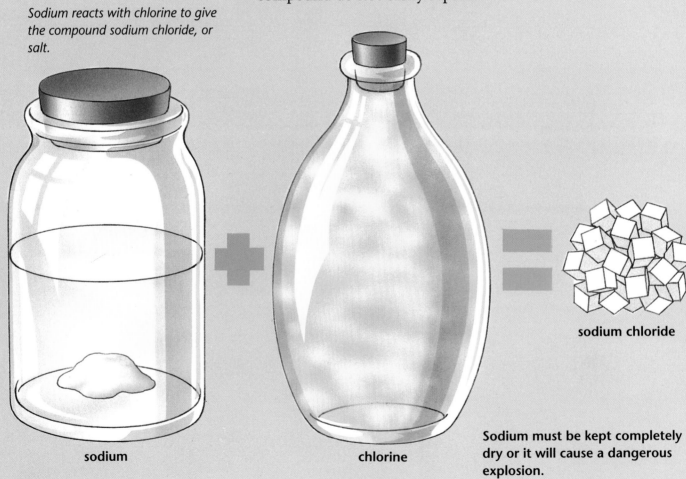

sodium

chlorine

sodium chloride

Sodium must be kept completely dry or it will cause a dangerous explosion.

Mixtures

A mixture is made up of two or more elements or compounds. Air is a mixture. It contains three main elements—oxygen, nitrogen, and argon. It also contains two compounds—carbon dioxide and water vapor.

Unlike a compound, a mixture can be easily separated into the substances it consists of. This is because these substances have not reacted together. For example, if you mix salt crystals with water and leave the mixture in a dish, the water will dry out, or **evaporate**, and salt crystals will be left behind.

Salt crystals dissolve in water to make a salt solution. When the water dries out, the salt crystals remain.

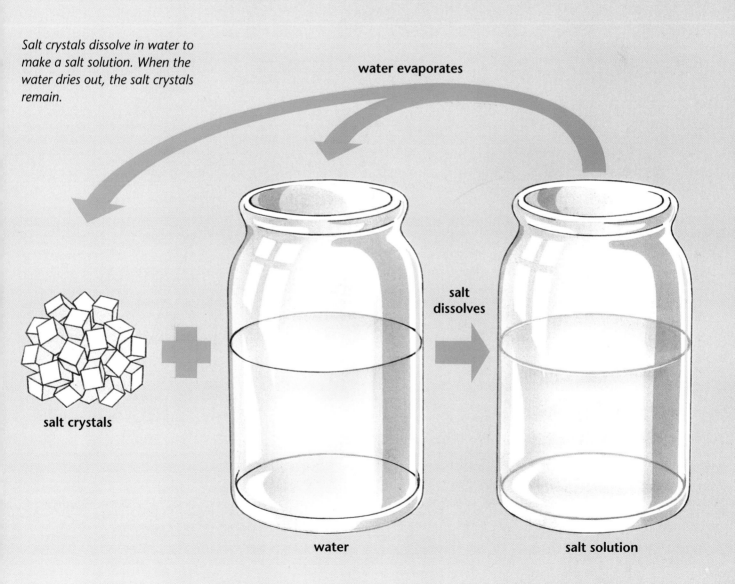

water evaporates

salt crystals

water

salt dissolves

salt solution

Crystal shapes

If you look very closely at some grains of salt, you will see that each grain has the same shape. Salt grains are shaped like tiny cubes. Regular shapes like this are called **crystals.** Many elements and compounds form crystals. The crystals in salt are easy to see. But other crystals are so small that you need to look through a microscope to see them.

The atoms in different crystals join together to form different patterns. There are seven basic patterns of crystal.

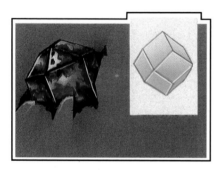

The atoms of garnet form isometric crystals.

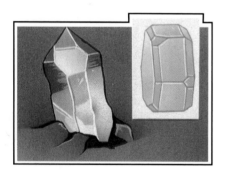

The atoms of quartz form rhombohedral crystals.

The atoms of zircon form tetragonal crystals.

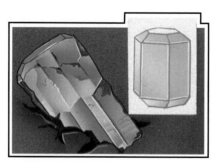

The atoms of beryl form hexagonal crystals.

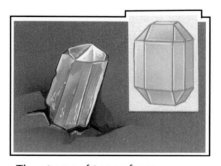

The atoms of topaz form orthorhombic crystals.

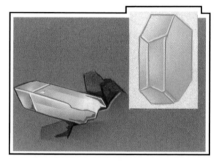

The atoms of gypsum form monoclinic crystals.

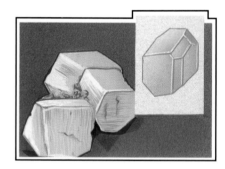

The atoms of feldspar form triclinic crystals.

How do crystals form?

Sugar and ice form as crystals. Many rocks and metals in Earth's surface are found as crystals, too. Crystals are made when liquids cool or solutions dry out. Some of the atoms move closer together. The crystals form in regular shapes because the atoms in the crystals arrange themselves in patterns. Crystals can grow larger over time as they attract more particles toward them. But each different crystal will always keep the same shape.

Atoms can be arranged in a variety of repeating patterns to make different crystals.

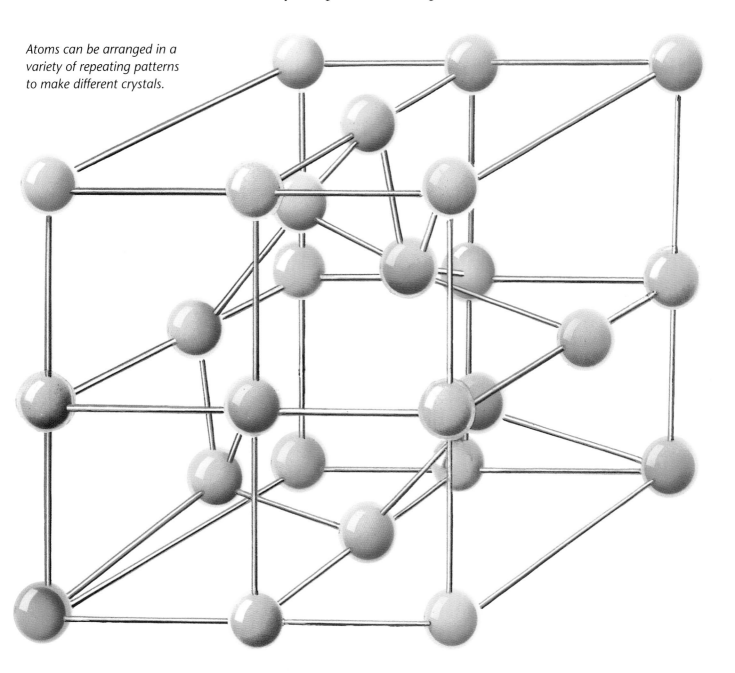

Acids and alkalis

Which drink do you prefer—lemonade or sweet tea? One is a weak acid and the other a weak alkali. If not for some sweetener, the lemonade would be a sour-tasting acid, and the tea a bitter-tasting alkali. Any substance that can be dissolved in water is either acidic or alkaline or, if neither, then neutral.

There are many different sorts of acids. Carbonated lemonade contains carbonic acid, and the hydrochloric acid in your stomach helps to digest your food. Car batteries are filled with sulfuric acid. Although these are all acids, they are not all the same strength. Carbonic acid is very weak and sulfuric acid is very strong. If you fill a car battery with lemonade, it certainly won't make enough electricity to start the engine!

There are also strong and weak alkalis. Bicarbonate of soda (baking soda) is a weak alkali used in cooking. Sodium hydroxide is a strong alkali that can clean baked-on grease from inside ovens. Scientists use an **indicator** to test the strength of an acid or an alkali. They add the indicator to a few drops of the substance they want to test. The color of the indicator changes. The color is checked against a color chart. This shows **pH numbers** between 1 and 14.

The pH (potential of hydrogen) number indicates the concentration of hydrogen ions in a solution. Strong acids are pH 1. They become weaker as the number rises to pH 6. Neutral substances are pH 7—neither acidic nor alkaline. Weak alkalis are pH 8. They become stronger as the number rises to pH 14.

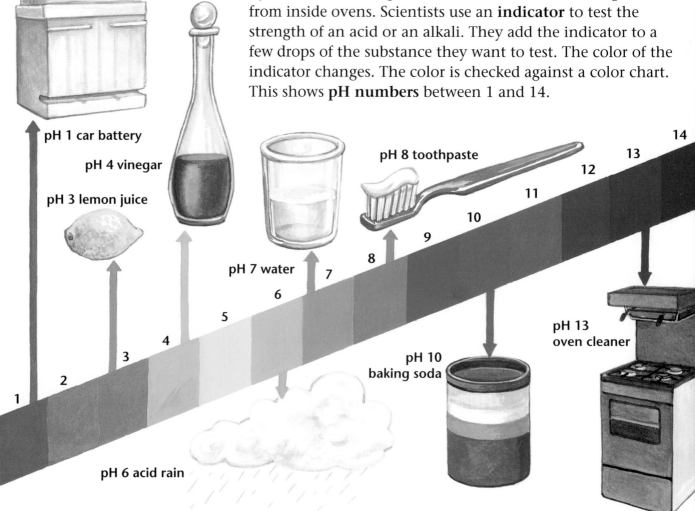

pH 1 car battery

pH 4 vinegar

pH 3 lemon juice

pH 7 water

pH 8 toothpaste

pH 6 acid rain

pH 10 baking soda

pH 13 oven cleaner

1 2 3 4 5 6 7 8 9 10 11 12 13 14

Balancing acids with alkalis

When you add an acid to an alkali, the alkaline substance and the acid balance each other out. Scientists say they **neutralize** each other. People can get indigestion pains when there is too much acid in their stomachs. Look at a packet of indigestion tablets. You'll see they contain bicarbonate of soda, also called baking soda or sodium bicarbonate. Why do you think this helps?

You will need:

red and blue litmus papers

6 glass jars

water

spoon for mixing

marker

labels

1 teaspoon lemon juice

1 teaspoon baking soda

1-inch (25-mm) "squeeze" of toothpaste

1 teaspoon vinegar

1-inch (25-mm) piece of chalk

Testing acids and alkalis

Find out if a solution is acidic or alkaline. The litmus papers are indicators.

1. Pour 1 inch (25 millimeters) of water into each jar. Mix one ingredient—the lemon juice, baking soda, toothpaste, vinegar, or chalk—into each of the jars. Leave one jar aside with just water.

2. Label each jar and line them up in the same order as the ingredients listed in the "You will need" list at left.

3. Place a litmus paper in each jar. What happens?

Acids turn the blue papers red. The red papers stay red in acids. Alkalis turn the red papers blue. The blue papers stay blue in alkalis. Neutral substances cause no reaction.

Solid, liquid, or gas

Our world is made of matter. Earth's crust is **solid**, the sea is **liquid**, and the air is a mixture of **gases.** Some matter, such as rocks and wood, are called solids. They don't change their shape. Lemonade and water are called liquids because they flow easily. If you pour a liquid into a container, it flows to fill up the shape of the container. The surface of the liquid is always level. Gases, like the air we breathe, spread to fill any space.

Substances remain as solids, liquids, or gases at certain temperatures. If they are heated or cooled, they change.

If you pour water into a container and leave it in the freezer of a refrigerator, the liquid water changes into ice, a solid. If you heat water until it boils, the liquid water becomes steam, a gas.

These Japanese macaque monkeys have found a hot, steamy pool to bathe in, even though there is snow on the ground. The water bubbles to the surface of the pool from deep inside the earth.

The molecules in ice do not move around much. They cling together to form a solid.

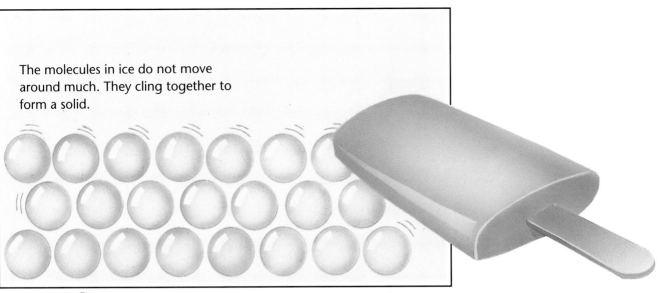

The molecules in liquid water move around freely.

When water becomes a gas, the molecules move quickly and spread out.

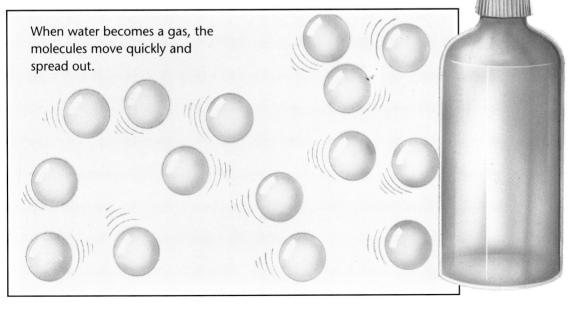

Melting and freezing

If you put some liquid water into the freezer, it soon turns into ice. When you take the ice out of the freezer, it melts back to liquid water again. Ice is solid water. Freezing water to make ice does not change the water into a different substance—it just changes the form of the water. Water changes to ice when the temperature falls below 32 °F (0 °C). Ice melts when the temperature rises above 32 °F (0 °C). This temperature is called the **freezing point** of water and the **melting point** of ice.

Melting

In ice and other solids, the particles are very close together and hardly move at all. This is why solids are hard and can't be squeezed into a smaller space. The particles are fixed in one place and although they do vibrate back and forth, they do not move away from each other. However, if you heat a solid, like ice, the particles vibrate faster and faster. Soon, the particles have a lot of energy. They are moving so fast that they break free from each other. When this happens, the solid melts into a liquid. The particles can now move about easily. This is what makes liquids flow.

The water on this plant has frozen overnight, when the temperature dropped below 32 °F (0 °C). As the temperature rises during the day, the ice will melt.

Freezing

As water cools, the particles lose energy and begin to slow down. When this happens, they move closer together. After a while, they are so close together that the liquid freezes and becomes a solid. Unlike most other substances, water **expands**, or takes up more space as it freezes. Most other substances, for example, gold and mercury, **contract**—take up less space—when frozen.

You will need:

empty pop bottle

very cold water

coin large enough to cover the opening of the bottle completely

Jumping molecules

Make this model to show what happens to the molecules in ice when it melts.

1. Rinse the empty pop bottle with very cold water or leave the bottle in the refrigerator for at least 10 minutes.

2. Spread some water over the lip of the bottle opening with your finger.

3. Place the coin over the wet lip of the bottle opening. After about three minutes, as the oxygen in the bottle warms and expands, the coin will click up and down. Try putting the bottle and coin in a sunny window. What happens?

Boiling point

What happens when water boils? Cold water heated in a kettle will boil after a few minutes. The temperature of the water keeps rising until it reaches 212 °F (100 °C). This is the **boiling point** of water. At this temperature, liquid water changes into a gas called **steam.** But why does boiling water turn into steam?

When water is a liquid, the molecules move around freely. They also hit each other and bounce apart again. Except at the surface, where the water slowly escapes into the air, the molecules can't escape from each other. Tiny amounts of electricity in the molecules hold them together. But as water heats up, energy is passed to the molecules, which move faster and faster. Eventually, when the water boils, the molecules near the surface have enough energy to escape rapidly out of the kettle.

⚠ **Be careful when handling boiling water! Do not put your hand** directly over the steam, or you could scald yourself.

If you boil water near a window, the steam from the kettle will condense in droplets on the pane.

You may find condensation on a glass window in the morning. Water vapor from the warm air inside the room cools during the night.

Evaporation and condensation

Water does not need to boil before it can turn into a gas. Even cold water in an uncovered glass will slowly change into a gas called **water vapor.** The water molecules gradually gain energy from the air. After a while, the molecules on the surface of the water have enough energy to break away from the other molecules. They become water vapor. This change from liquid to gas is called **evaporation.**

Have you noticed water running down the window panes when the water in a kettle is boiling? The molecules of water in the steam hit the cold air on the surface of the glass and cool down. As they lose energy, the molecules slow down and move much closer together, becoming water. The steam has turned back into a liquid. This is called **condensation.**

Taking up space

Look at some aerosol cans. Many of these have a warning printed on them. They warn us not to heat the can or throw it into a fire. This is because there is a gas inside the can. When a gas is heated, it expands to take up more space. If there is no way for the gas to escape, the can will explode. When a gas cools, it contracts to take up less space.

You will need:

modeling clay

a drinking straw

a glass bottle

a bowl of water

a cloth

Warming air and water

You can try this experiment to show what happens when you warm air and water.

1. Using modeling clay, seal a drinking straw into the neck of a glass bottle. Hold the bottle upside down and dip the end of the straw into a bowl of water.

2. Now wrap a warm, wet cloth around the bottle to heat the air inside. What is escaping from the end of the straw? Explain why.

Hot and cold air

Why does hot air take up more space than cold air? Air is a mixture of gases. Heating the air puts more energy into these gases. The tiny particles of gas rush about faster and faster and hit each other more often. The particles bounce off each other and push out to take up more space. So the gas expands.

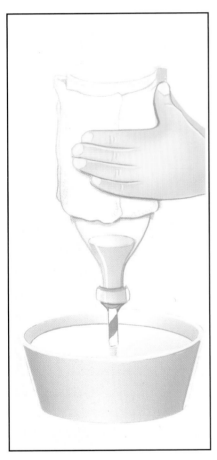

3. Now replace the warm, wet cloth with a cold one. What happens to the air inside the bottle? Describe what you see. Explain.

4. This time, fill the bottle with cold water before you fit the straw. Some of the water should rise a little way up the straw. Now stand the bottle in a bowl of hot water to heat the water inside the bottle. What happens? Explain.

The particles in a liquid are not rushing about as fast as the particles in a gas. They slide past each other and hit each other less often than the particles in a gas. But warming a liquid makes the particles move faster, making the liquid expand.

⚠️

Work carefully with hot water.

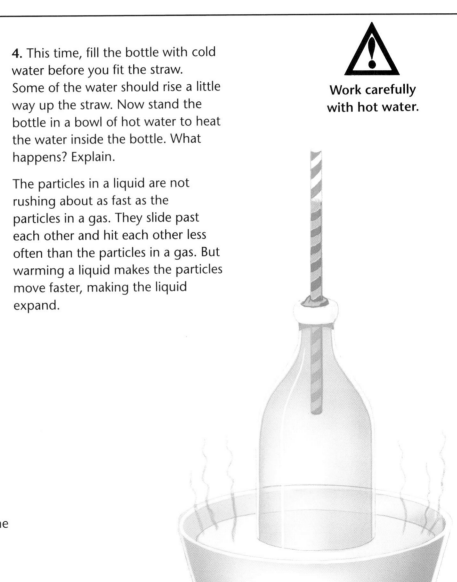

Invisible changes

If you look at sugar through a magnifying glass, you will see white or brown crystals of sugar. If you heat the sugar, it will melt and bubble. When it cools, a hard, glassy candy is left. Many substances change into something new when they are heated. Other substances don't change at all when they are heated. Sand is not changed by the heat from an ordinary flame. Scientists can make sand melt, but they have to raise the temperature to over 2732 °F (1500 °C).

Some substances appear to stay the same when you heat them. Bicarbonate of soda (baking soda) is a white powder. When you heat it, it remains a white powder. From just looking at it, you would think that the bicarbonate of soda has not changed. But an invisible change has taken place.

Chemists use a balance to measure changes that cannot be seen.

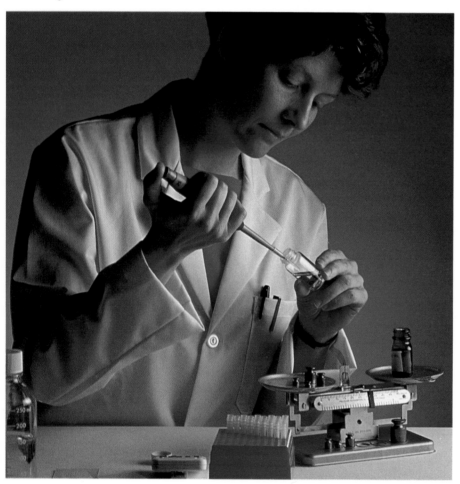

You will need:

baking soda

a teaspoon

rice

two small wooden blocks and a match

a drinking straw

aluminum foil

a large needle

Never handle matches
or needles unless an adult
is with you.

Find out more by looking
at pages **36–37**

Can you believe your eyes?

Find out how bicarbonate of soda (baking soda) changes when
it is heated. This balancing machine will help you to see if two
samples weigh the same after
one sample has been heated.
Ask an adult to help you.

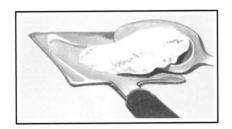

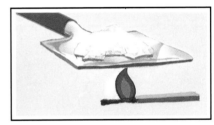

1. Use the drinking straw, the two
wooden blocks, the aluminum foil,
and the needle to make a balance as
shown in the picture. Ask an adult to
poke the needle through the middle
of the straw.

2. Place one teaspoonful of baking
soda on one side of your balance.
Add just enough grains of rice to
the other side so that the two sides
are balanced.

3. Now ask an adult to burn half
the length of a match under the
bicarbonate of soda. This will take
about five seconds.

At the start, the rice and the
soda weighed the same. After
heating, the bicarbonate of soda
weighs less. The rice is now heavier.
So what happened? The baking
soda gave off an invisible gas when
heated, reducing its weight.

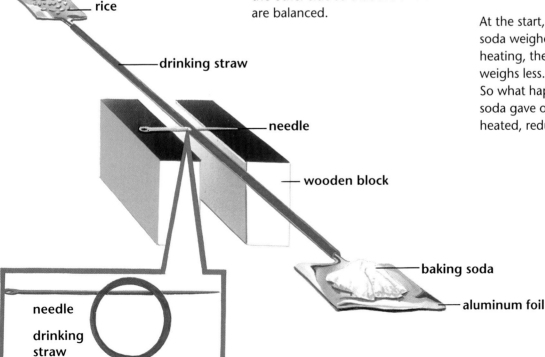

rice

drinking straw

needle

wooden block

baking soda

aluminum foil

needle

drinking
straw

Find out more by looking at pages **38–39**

Heating and changing

Many substances will change if they are heated. Ice will melt into water if it takes in enough heat and the temperature rises above 32 °F (0 °C). Even solid iron can melt into a liquid. But the temperature must be many times higher than boiling water—above 3000 °F (1600 °C).

Temporary changes

Liquid water and liquid iron can both change back to solids again when the temperature is low enough. Changes like this are called **physical changes**. They are **temporary** because they are reversible. In other words, you can always get back to the substance you started with.

Testing changes

You can do your own experiments to discover more about temporary and permanent changes. **Ask an adult to help you.**

You will need:

aluminum foil

scissors

matches

magnifying glass

substances to be tested, such as:

    salt

    sugar

    baking soda

    sand

    paper

    wax

    wood

1. Cut a strip of aluminum foil.

2. Crumple the foil into the shape of a spoon.

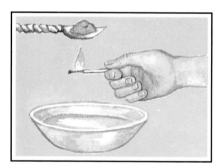

3. Put a small amount of the substance to be tested in the foil spoon. Ask your adult helper to hold a lighted match underneath the spoon, and see what happens.

Permanent changes

Heat can also make substances change in a **permanent** way so that they can't be changed back again. If you leave a slice of bread in the toaster too long, the result is a lump of a smoking, black substance called carbon. It would be impossible to turn the carbon and the smoke back into a slice of bread. Cars burn gasoline as a fuel. The gasoline burns in the engine to make the car travel down the road. After the gasoline is burned, exhaust gases come out of the tailpipe. The exhaust gases can't be turned back into gasoline. Changes like this are called **chemical changes.** They are permanent.

Be very careful when heating something. Always ask an adult to help. Hold the foil and match over a bowl of water so that you can safely drop them into the water if they become too hot.

What happened?

When each experiment is finished, use your notebook to record your results. After all the experiments, review your findings. Which substances have not changed at all? Which samples have changed permanently, and which have changed temporarily? You can make a chart that summarizes the results.

Compare the heated substances with some fresh, unheated substances. Look at the substances through a magnifying glass. Try stirring the heated remains with the end of a used matchstick to see what is left.

Many scientists working in laboratories use heat to discover new and useful substances. Heating is a good way of making changes happen.

Frothing and fizzing

All sorts of things can happen when you mix two substances together. Try mixing sand and water. The sand sinks to the bottom of the glass. But if you mix salt with water, the salt seems to disappear. When you mix some substances together, the mixture begins to froth and fizz. Mixing substances can change them or even produce a new substance.

You will need:

a glass jar with a lid

a saucer

some baking soda

some vinegar

matches

Making gas

Try mixing baking soda and vinegar.

1. Pour vinegar into the glass jar to a depth of about $1/2$ inch (1.25 centimeters).

2. Now put in a teaspoonful of baking soda and quickly cover the jar. What happens? Use your notebook to record your observations.

3. Now add some more baking soda. What happens this time? Is the reaction the same? Explain.

4. Ask an adult to lift the cover off the jar and slowly place a burning match inside it. Does the match stay lit or go out?

Never handle matches unless an adult is with you.

What happened?

The jar was full of air before the reaction. The gas made by the reaction filled the jar and pushed the air out. The name of this new gas is **carbon dioxide.** The flame went out because it can't burn in carbon dioxide.

Vinegar is a very weak acid, containing a chemical called **acetic acid.** Acetic acid is also present in lemons and other citrus fruits. It is acetic acid that gives vinegar and citrus their sharp taste.

Testing with lemon juice

Do you think that a different acid will make the baking soda fizz and froth? Lemons have a sharp acid taste so perhaps lemon juice will work.

1. Put some lemon juice into your glass jar and add enough water so that the liquid is ¹/₂ inch (1.25 centimeters) deep.

2. Now do the tests as before. Lemon juice contains citric acid— so you should expect similar results.

Fast and slow changes

Over many years, a gleaming new car changes into a rusty old wreck. The car is made from steel, which contains the metal iron. Oxygen and water from the air react with the iron to make brown crumbly rust. When one substance changes into another substance, or substances, we say that a **chemical reaction** has taken place. Some chemical reactions, like rusting, take place fairly slowly.

Other chemical changes happen more quickly. When gunpowder is ignited, it reacts with air to form gases. This reaction takes a split second. The gases are made so quickly that they rush outward at an enormous speed. You can see the effects of the fast chemical reaction between gunpowder and air when you watch a fireworks display.

Very quick chemical reactions send fireworks high up into the air.

A slow chemical reaction has turned this car rusty.

Speeding up a chemical reaction

In this experiment, chalk and vinegar are mixed together. This causes a chemical reaction. Carbon dioxide gas is given off while the chalk dissolves. There are three ways in which you can make the reaction happen more quickly. If you heat the vinegar and chalk mixture, the carbon dioxide will come bubbling up more quickly. If you use powdered chalk, the reaction will be faster. Strong vinegar reacts faster than watery vinegar.

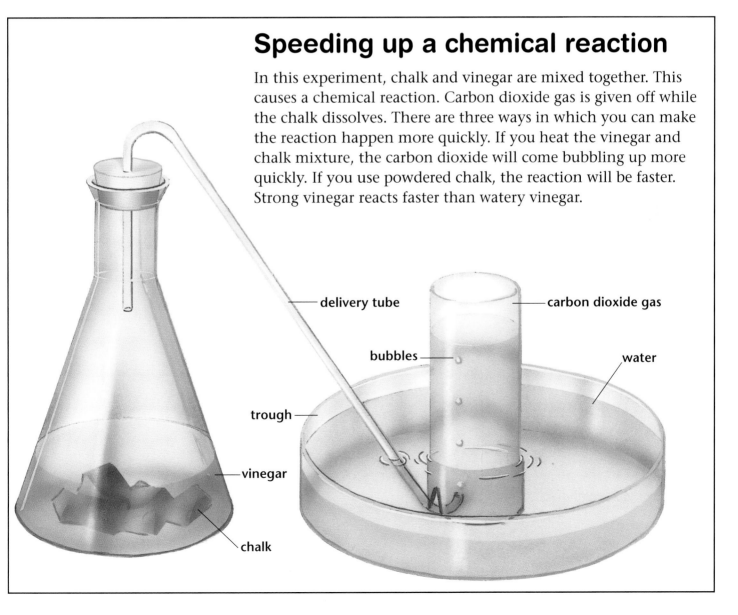

delivery tube

carbon dioxide gas

bubbles

water

trough

vinegar

chalk

Making new materials

Mixing things with acids and alkalis often causes chemical reactions. The result of these chemical reactions is often a new material. These materials can be useful in industry for making new products or improving products that already exist.

A useful acid

Sulfuric acid is a very dangerous liquid. It is one of the strongest acids. This clear, oily liquid is strong enough to eat through most metals. Yet it is used when producing many of the familiar goods you can buy in stores, from paper to iron objects. Sulfuric acid is made from sulfur, a substance found alone in nature as a yellow solid or in combination with oil or many minerals. Sulfur, oxygen, and water react together to make sulfuric acid.

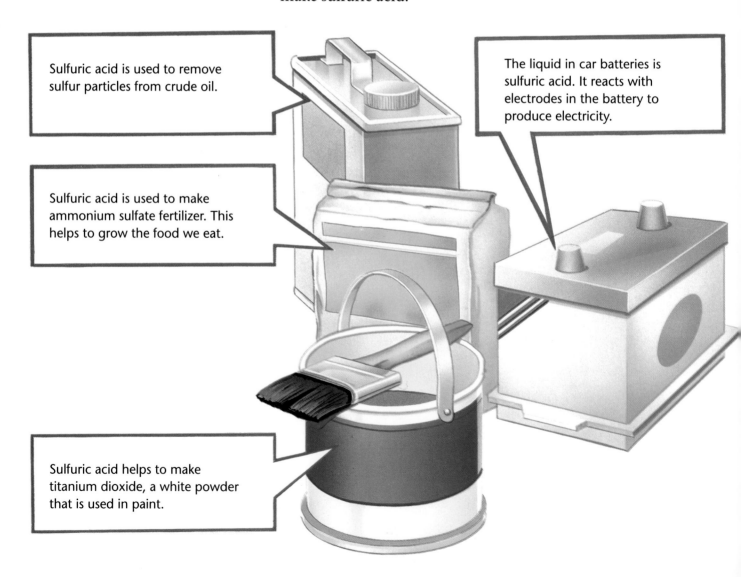

Sulfuric acid is used to remove sulfur particles from crude oil.

The liquid in car batteries is sulfuric acid. It reacts with electrodes in the battery to produce electricity.

Sulfuric acid is used to make ammonium sulfate fertilizer. This helps to grow the food we eat.

Sulfuric acid helps to make titanium dioxide, a white powder that is used in paint.

A useful alkali

Sodium carbonate is a white powder or crystal. It is an alkali, which means that it neutralizes acid. Sodium carbonate helps to make many different products, from glass to food and drink. Because sodium carbonate can kill many kinds of germs, it is also an important disinfectant and household cleaner.

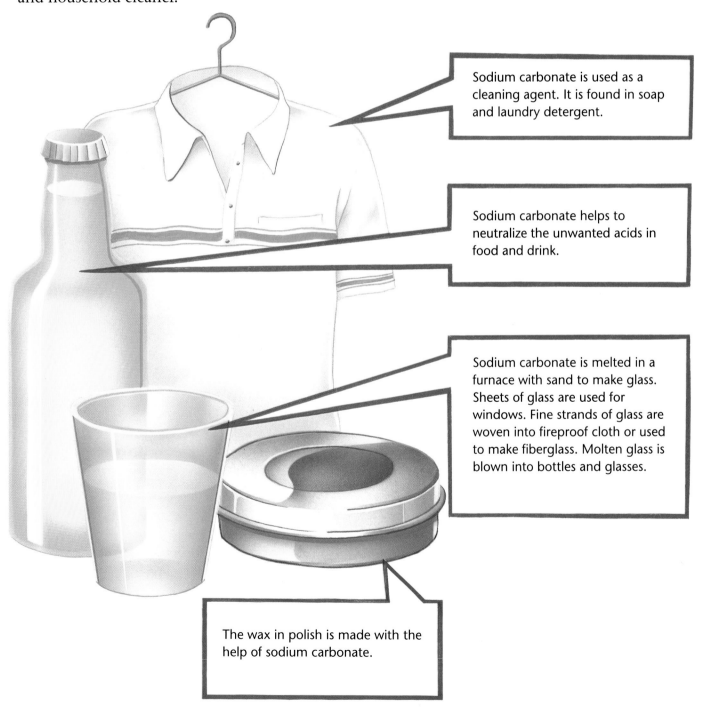

Sodium carbonate is used as a cleaning agent. It is found in soap and laundry detergent.

Sodium carbonate helps to neutralize the unwanted acids in food and drink.

Sodium carbonate is melted in a furnace with sand to make glass. Sheets of glass are used for windows. Fine strands of glass are woven into fireproof cloth or used to make fiberglass. Molten glass is blown into bottles and glasses.

The wax in polish is made with the help of sodium carbonate.

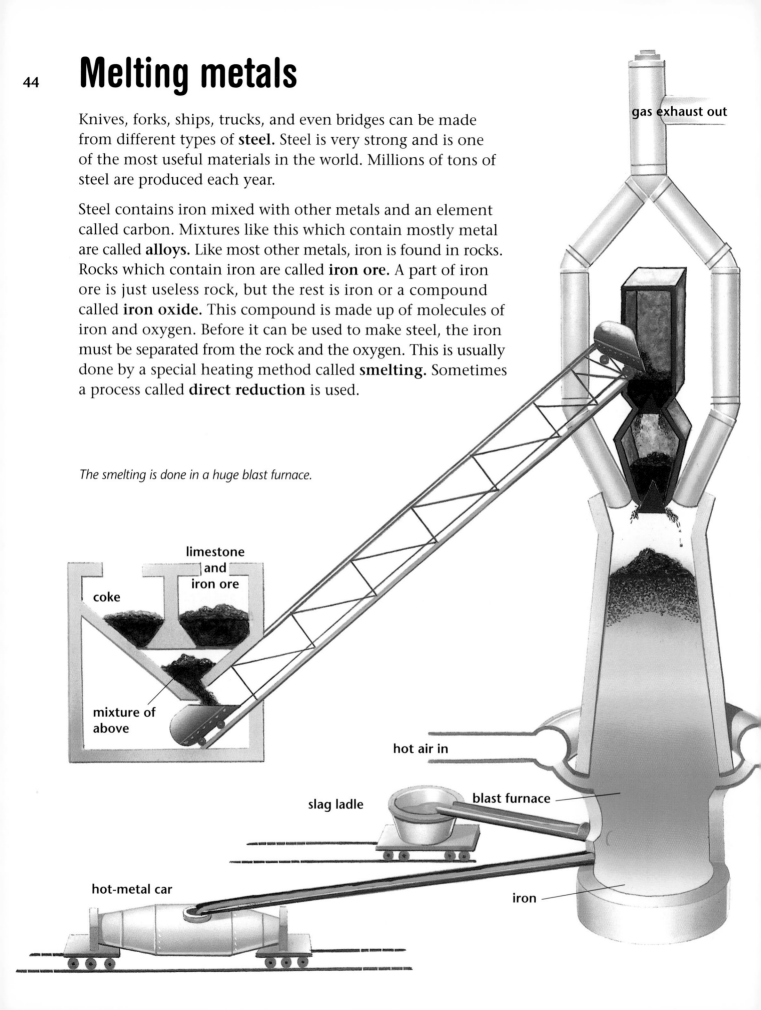

Melting metals

Knives, forks, ships, trucks, and even bridges can be made from different types of **steel**. Steel is very strong and is one of the most useful materials in the world. Millions of tons of steel are produced each year.

Steel contains iron mixed with other metals and an element called carbon. Mixtures like this which contain mostly metal are called **alloys**. Like most other metals, iron is found in rocks. Rocks which contain iron are called **iron ore**. A part of iron ore is just useless rock, but the rest is iron or a compound called **iron oxide**. This compound is made up of molecules of iron and oxygen. Before it can be used to make steel, the iron must be separated from the rock and the oxygen. This is usually done by a special heating method called **smelting**. Sometimes a process called **direct reduction** is used.

The smelting is done in a huge blast furnace.

gas exhaust out

limestone
and
iron ore

coke

mixture of
above

hot air in

slag ladle

blast furnace

hot-metal car

iron

What happens in smelting?

Iron ore is mixed with limestone and coke. The mixture is tipped into the top of a blast furnace. A blast of hot air is blown into the bottom of the furnace. The coke, which is made from coal, burns easily and soon becomes very hot. A gas called carbon monoxide results. The carbon monoxide takes oxygen from the iron oxide. This reaction produces iron and another gas called carbon dioxide.

The iron then melts in the strong heat and trickles down to the bottom of the furnace. At the same time, the rock in the iron ore reacts with the heated limestone to make another liquid mixture called **slag**. This pours out separately and is sometimes used to make cement. The liquid iron is taken away to be cleaned and mixed with other liquid metals. The resulting mixture then hardens into steel.

Liquid iron is poured into hot-metal cars. These cars are taken on rails to another part of the steel mill, where the liquid iron is cleaned.

Salty water and electricity

Electricity flows easily through metal wires. Copper, aluminum, and silver are good conductors of electricity. Electricity can also flow easily through some salt, acid, or alkaline solutions. When electricity flows through a solution, the solution is changed by the flow of electricity, and new substances are produced.

Always be very careful when working with electrical parts.

You will need:

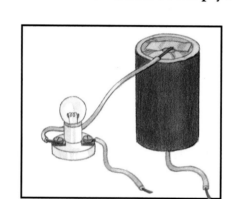

three pieces of thin, plastic-coated wire, each 6 in. (15 cm) long, with bare ends

a 1.5-volt (D) battery

a 1.5-volt bulb in a bulb holder

electrical tape

a glass of very salty water

New substances from salty water

Salt crystals dissolve easily in water, and this solution is a good conductor of electricity. Here is an experiment to show this. **Ask an adult to help you.**

1. Connect the wires to the battery and the bulb as shown.

2. Now place the two free ends in the salt solution. The wires that dip into the solution are called the electrodes.

You will see bubbles of gas collect on both the electrodes, and you will notice a smell, like bleach. The electricity has made a chemical reaction happen. The salt solution has given off two gases—chlorine, which you can smell, and hydrogen. The new salt solution is called sodium hydroxide.

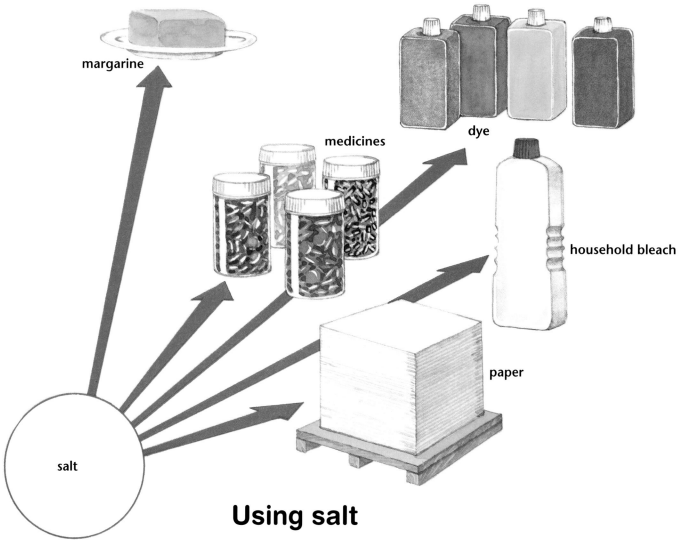

margarine

medicines

dye

household bleach

paper

salt

Many new substances can be produced from salty water. These are so useful that millions of tons of them are used each year in industry. They help to make a wide range of products, such as foods, medicines, and clothing.

Using salt

Salt is one of the most important substances in industry. When an electric current is passed through a salt solution, three very useful substances are produced. These are chlorine, hydrogen, and sodium hydroxide. These three substances are so important that millions of tons of salty water are broken down each year using electricity. Deep under the ground in some parts of the world are enormous layers of solid salt. One method for removing the salt is to drill holes down to these layers. Water is then pumped down some holes, and salt solution comes up through others. This solution contains far more dissolved salt than seawater.

Electricity is passed through the salty water in special tanks to produce the chlorine, hydrogen, and sodium hydroxide. Chlorine can be combined with hydrogen to produce hydrochloric acid. Chlorine and sodium hydroxide also react together, producing a chemical compound called sodium hypochlorite. So a total of five new substances can be made.

Making coats of metal

If you pass electricity through a solution, you can cause a chemical reaction. New substances are produced where the electric current enters and leaves the solution—at the **electrodes.** Electricity can also change the electrodes themselves. Here is an experiment you can try.

Ask an adult to help you with this experiment.

You will need:

a small glass jar, filled with vinegar

two plastic-coated, copper wires, each about 12 in. (30 cm) long

a piece of lead for a mechanical pencil, about 2 in. (5 cm) long

a 1.5-volt (D) battery

electrical tape

How to make copper move through vinegar

Make your own chemical reaction using electricity.

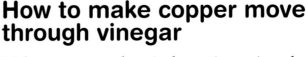

1. Take the two coated wires and carefully cut ¹/₂ inch (1.25 centimeters) of the plastic coating from three ends.

2. Cut 4 inches (10 centimeters) of the coating from the fourth end, and bend the bare copper wire into a U shape. Now connect the other piece of wire to the pencil lead.

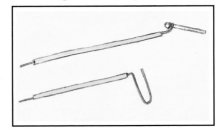

3. Join the two free ends to the battery. Connect the other end of the wire with the pencil lead to the negative (−) terminal of the battery. Connect the other end of the piece of wire with the U-shape to the positive (+) terminal. These are the electrodes.

4. Put the pencil lead and the U-shaped wire into the vinegar. Move these two electrodes closer together until you notice bubbles in the vinegar. Move them apart again until the bubbles stop.

These copper kettles are first dipped into a green nickel bath and then an orange chrome bath.

5. Move the two electrodes close together again until you notice the bubbles. After about 10 minutes, disconnect the battery and take the electrodes out of the vinegar. What changes do you notice? (See answer below.)

The copper wire is cleaner and brighter than before, and the pencil lead has a grayish or pinkish-brown coat. The electric current has taken copper from the U-shaped wire through the solution, and coated it onto the pencil lead.

6. Now you can make the coating disappear again! Put your electrodes back into the vinegar. This time connect the pencil lead to the positive (+) connection and the U-shaped wire to the negative (−) connection.

How is electroplating used?

The method of making a metal coating by means of electricity is called **electroplating**. It is often used to put very thin coats of expensive metals, like silver or gold, onto cheaper metals. Most gold watches are really made from a mixture of other metals with just a thin electroplating of gold on the surface. Some knives, forks, and spoons are stamped with the letters EPNS. This stands for Electroplated Nickel Silver. The silver coating gives them a bright, shiny surface.

Sometimes metals are coated for protection. Many machines are made from iron and steel, but these metals rust in damp air. **Chromium** metal does not rust but is very expensive. So small amounts of chromium are used to electroplate the surfaces of these cheaper metals. This makes them look better and last much longer.

Making pure aluminum

Like many metals, aluminum is a very useful element. It is found in rock as **bauxite**, which is an aluminum ore containing oxygen. The oxygen has to be removed before the aluminum can be used. But the oxygen and the aluminum are joined so firmly that ordinary smelting does not remove the oxygen as it does with other metals. The best way to separate the aluminum and the oxygen is to pass electricity through them. This is called **electrolysis.**

First, rock and sandy particles are removed from the aluminum ore. This leaves a white powder called **aluminum oxide.** It is made up of aluminum atoms joined to oxygen atoms. The powder is dissolved in a tank of chemicals and heated to about 1742 °F (950 °C). This makes the aluminum oxide melt and become a liquid.

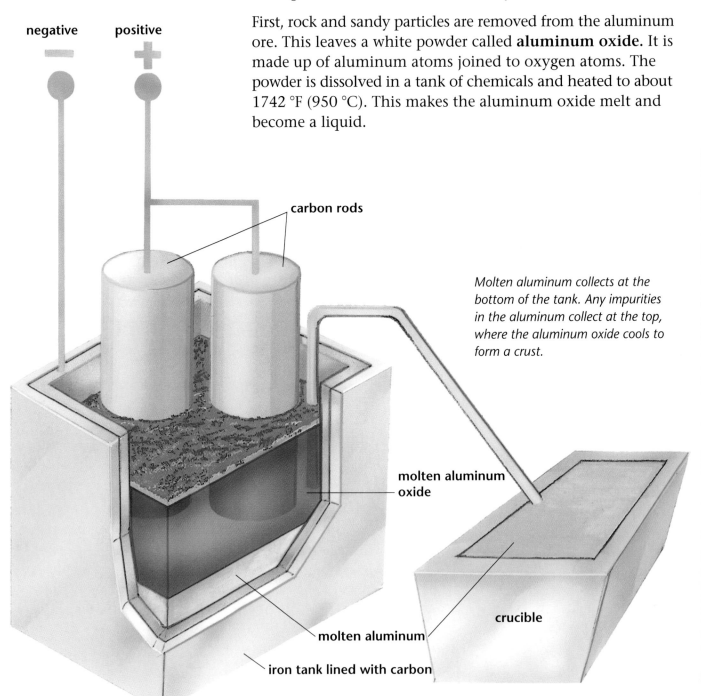

negative   positive

carbon rods

Molten aluminum collects at the bottom of the tank. Any impurities in the aluminum collect at the top, where the aluminum oxide cools to form a crust.

molten aluminum oxide

molten aluminum

iron tank lined with carbon

crucible

The power of electrolysis

Rods made of carbon are lowered into the molten aluminum oxide. An electric current flows through the molten liquid. The current enters the liquid through one of the rods and leaves through the carbon lining of the tank. As this happens, the current breaks up the molten aluminum oxide into aluminum and oxygen. The molten aluminum metal sinks to the bottom of the tank, and the oxygen combines with the carbon, to be released as carbon dioxide gas.

The pure, molten aluminum is drawn off into a crucible and then poured into molds to cool. The cool aluminum hardens into ingots.

The molten aluminum is drawn off into a crucible and poured into casting molds to cool and harden.

Taking gases from the air

Air is a mixture of many different gases. These different gases are very useful. But they must be separated from each other before we can put them to use.

Air is first changed from a gas to a liquid. It is **compressed**, which means it is squeezed into a smaller space, and then cooled to about $-310\,°F$ ($-190\,°C$). Then the liquid air passes into a tower called a **fractionating column.** The tower is warmer at the bottom and cooler at the top. The liquid begins to evaporate, turning into gas. Some gases evaporate at a lower temperature. Helium and neon collect at the top of the tower. Nitrogen evaporates next, leaving liquid oxygen at the bottom of the tower. Separating gases in this way is called **fractional distillation.**

air

liquid air

1. The air contains many different gases. If you could divide the air into parts, you would find large amounts of nitrogen, oxygen, and water vapor. There are smaller amounts of argon and carbon dioxide, and even smaller amounts of other gases.

2. The air is filtered and compressed in a tank. Carbon dioxide and water vapor are removed from the air before it is cooled.

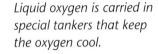

What are the gases used for?

Gases from the air are used in many different ways. People with breathing problems cannot take in enough oxygen. They are given special air with extra oxygen added to it. Fuels cannot burn without oxygen. A gas called acetylene burns in pure oxygen to make a very hot flame. The flame can melt metals and cut through them. In sewage plants, oxygen is used to help change harmful substances into harmless ones.

Liquid nitrogen is very cold and is used to freeze foods quickly. It can also freeze liquids in damaged pipes so that the pipes can be repaired. Substances do not burn in nitrogen, so it is also used inside light bulbs to keep the filament from burning away. In oil tankers, it can prevent fires and explosions. Plants need nitrogen, so many farmers put fertilizers containing nitrogen compounds into the soil.

Liquid oxygen is carried in special tankers that keep the oxygen cool.

fractionating column

3. The cool liquid air is passed into a large tower. As the liquid warms, the gases separate into different layers.

A column of oil

Crude oil is a mixture of many different chemicals called **hydrocarbons.** Hydrocarbons are useful because they can be used to make many different substances, such as butane gas, gasoline and diesel fuel, plastics, medicines, and paints.

Before crude oil can be used, it has to be refined. In the refinery, the crude oil is heated and turned into a mixture of gases and liquids. The mixture is then passed into a huge fractionating column. Inside the column, there are trays at different levels. The column is hotter at the bottom and cooler at the top. The gases pass up the column and condense into liquids on the trays at different temperatures. The gases that have longer molecules, with more carbon atoms, condense at higher temperatures. Those with shorter molecules and fewer carbon atoms condense at lower temperatures. This process is another example of fractional distillation.

Every day, thousands of tons of oil are turned into useful substances at large refineries.

Different hydrocarbons have different numbers of carbon atoms.

Hydrocarbons with 1 to 5 carbon atoms remain as gas at the top of the column. The gas is used as bottled fuel.

Gasoline has 5 to 10 carbon atoms and is used as fuel for cars.

Naphtha has 8 to 12 carbon atoms and is used to make chemicals.

Kerosene has 9 to 16 carbon atoms and is used as jet fuel.

Diesel oil has 15 to 25 carbon atoms and is used as fuel for trains and ships.

Bitumen has over 20 carbon atoms and is used for sealing roofs.

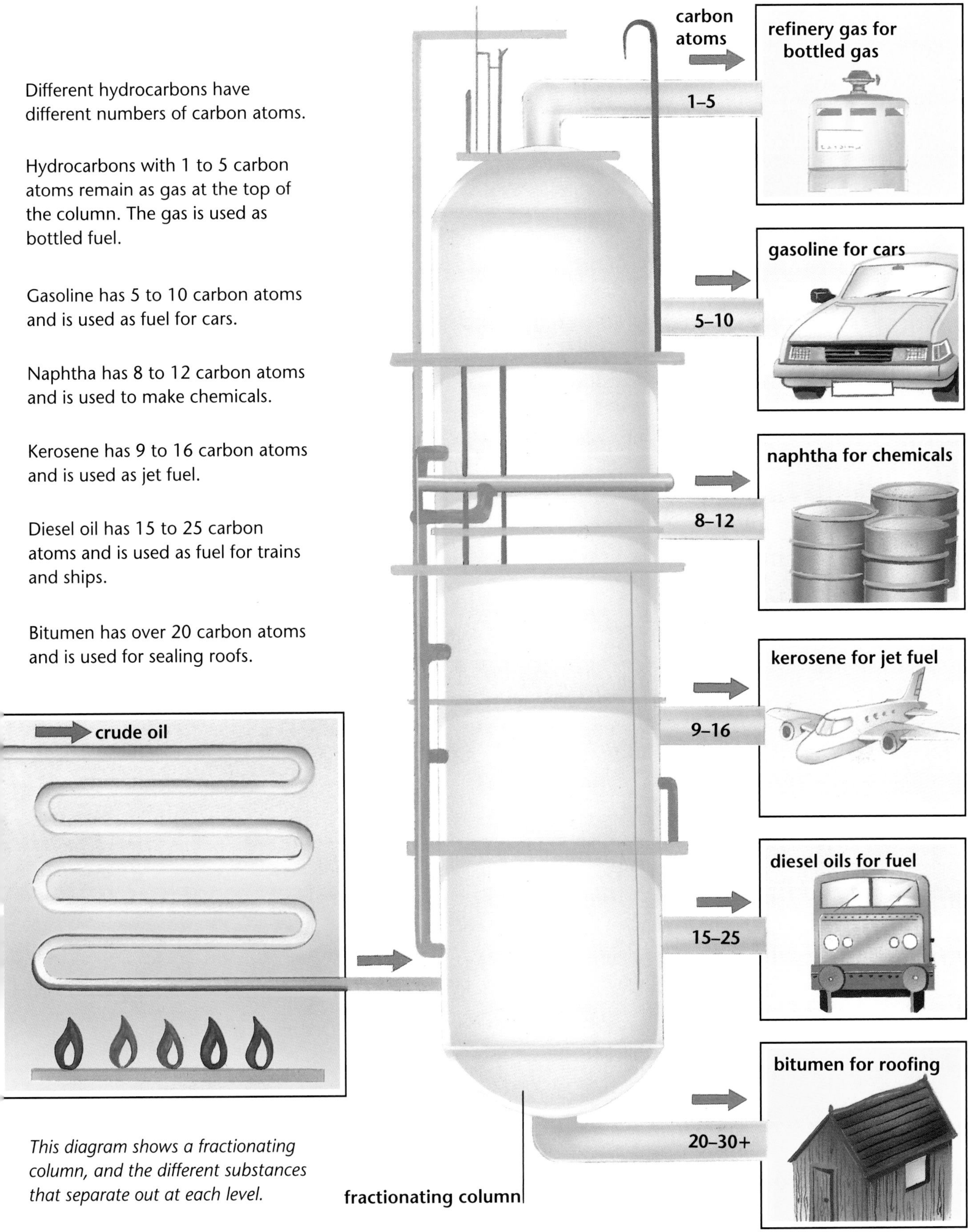

crude oil

This diagram shows a fractionating column, and the different substances that separate out at each level.

carbon atoms

refinery gas for bottled gas

1–5

gasoline for cars

5–10

naphtha for chemicals

8–12

kerosene for jet fuel

9–16

diesel oils for fuel

15–25

bitumen for roofing

20–30+

fractionating column

Plastics

Take a look around you. How many things can you see made from plastics? In our modern world, different kinds of plastics are everywhere. Some people even have pieces of plastic in their bodies, such as valves inside their hearts, or joints in knees and hips.

Plastics are **synthetic**, which means they are not natural, but have been invented by scientists. Polyvinyl chloride, or PVC for short, is used to make toys, pipes, and raincoats. Another type of plastic, polytetrafluoroethylene, PTFE, is used to coat the inside of nonstick saucepans. Many pens are made from a plastic called polystyrene. Polyethylene terephthalate (PET) is a type of polyester used to make a type of beverage bottle.

Many everyday products contain plastics.

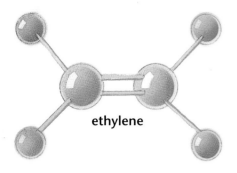

ethylene

Ethylene is a hydrocarbon. Its molecules are called **monomers.** Ethylene monomers can be joined together with the help of a catalyst to form longer molecules called polymers.

How are plastics made?

Most plastics are made from chemicals taken from crude oil. In an oil refinery, oil is separated into several different substances. One of them is a hydrocarbon called **ethylene.** The molecules of a hydrocarbon combine into long chains called **polymers.** A special chemical called a **catalyst** is needed to make this happen.

Making polyethylene

When scientists combine ethylene molecules, they make a polymer called **polyethylene.** Polyethylene is a plastic that is used to make bottles and containers. By adding different catalysts to different hydrocarbons, other kinds of plastics can be made.

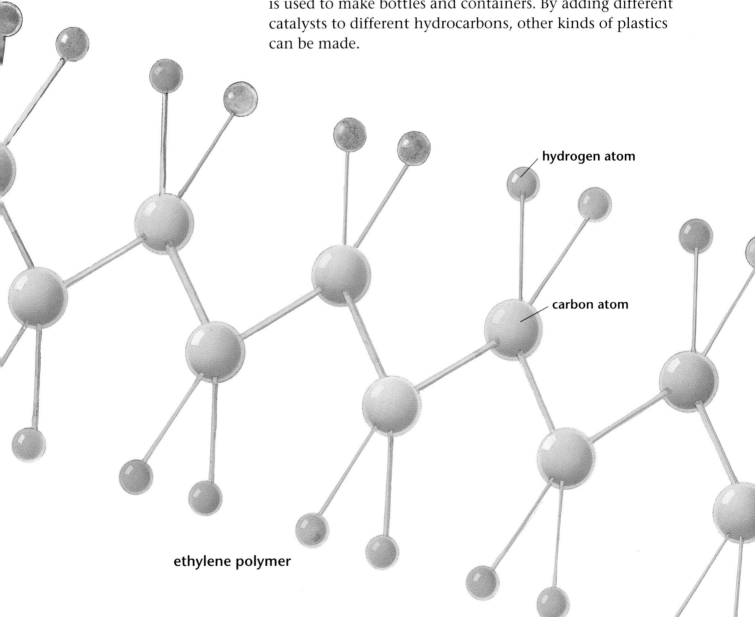

hydrogen atom

carbon atom

ethylene polymer

Rubber and latex

Think of all the different things that can be made from rubber. There are gloves, rubber bands, boots and shoes, fan belts for cars, inflatable boats, bottle stoppers, balls, tires, and foam mattresses. The rubber used to make each of these items is different. Some rubber is light and spongy, some is stretchy, and some is hard and stiff. Imagine a mattress made from the rubber in a bottle stopper. It would be very uncomfortable!

Most rubber is synthetic, or artificially made. Natural rubber is made from a white liquid called **latex**. It is the sap that comes from rubber trees. A V shape is cut in the bark of the tree. The sticky, white latex oozes from the cut and is collected in small cups tied to the tree trunk.

Latex is made of long chains of carbon and hydrogen atoms joined together. These are called **hydrocarbons.** The long hydrocarbons can easily slide past each other while latex is a liquid.

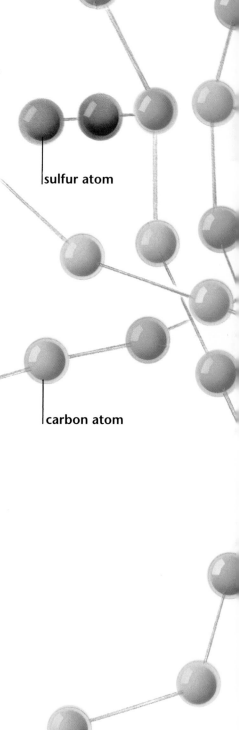

sulfur atom

carbon atom

Sticky, white latex is collected from rubber trees. The latex contains rubber.

Sheets of rubber are wrapped around a drum to make tires for cars, tractors, and bicycles.

Strengthening rubber

To make latex into a useful, springy solid, it is heated with a substance called sulfur. The sulfur atoms make bridges between the hydrocarbons and lock them together. This type of rubber, called vulcanized rubber, is very tough. It is used to make tires.

Vulcanized rubber is a good example of how scientists are able to take hydrocarbons, and many other basic building blocks of matter, and rearrange them to make new materials that are stronger, stiffer, softer, or more elastic.

When rubber is heated with sulfur, the sulfur combines with the hydrocarbons in the rubber. This process is called vulcanization.

Invisible rays

The world is changing around us all the time. Matter changes its form from solid to liquid to gas. When water evaporates, the water molecules stay the same but move farther apart.

There are chemical changes, too, such as iron rusting. When iron atoms combine with oxygen atoms and water, they react together to become a different substance.

There is another way in which matter changes. Matter can go through a **nuclear change.** When a nuclear change happens, the nucleus of the atom sends out invisible particles and rays. Substances that contain this type of atom are called **radioactive** substances.

How strong is radioactivity?

Radioactive substances send out three main kinds of radiation. A beam of **alpha particles** is not strong enough to pass through two pieces of strong paper. A beam of **beta particles** can pass through paper but can be blocked by a thin sheet of aluminum. **Gamma rays** can pass through a concrete wall. Only a thick layer of lead can stop the path of a gamma ray.

Matter contains some radioactive atoms. They can be both harmful and useful.

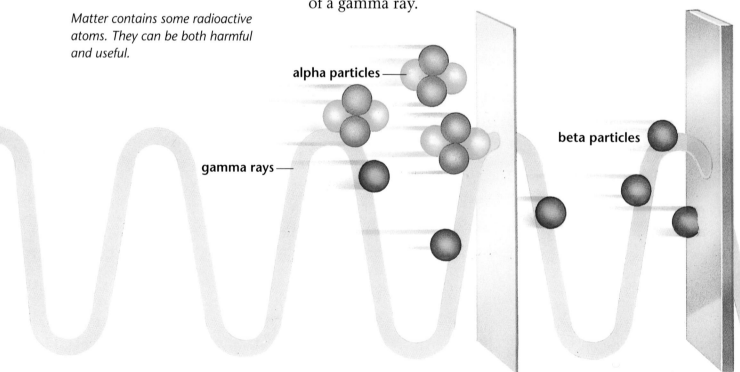

alpha particles

gamma rays

beta particles

paper

aluminum

There are many ways in which radioactive substances and radiation are used in medicine. Radiation therapy, shown right, attacks cancers with X rays or particles from radioactive substances.

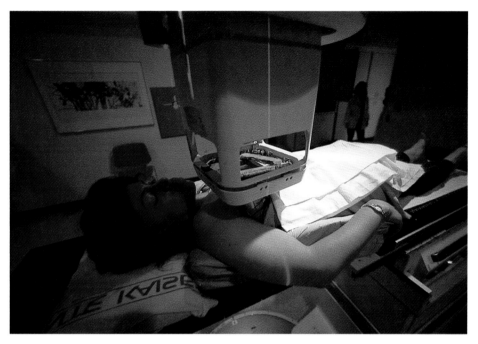

Using radioactivity

A gamma ray can be used to check metal pipes and machine parts for cracks. A photograph is taken as the ray passes through the metal and strikes photographic film.

A beam of beta particles can be used to check if packages are full or empty. If the package is empty, the beam will pass all the way through it.

Materials contain small amounts of radioactive atoms. In time, these atoms gradually change into different kinds of substances and the radioactivity decays. Scientists can measure the age of rocks and fossils, bones, and even ancient cloth by measuring the amount of radioactivity left in the material. This is called **radiocarbon dating**.

Is radioactivity harmful?

Although radioactivity can be very useful, it can also be very dangerous. If people are exposed to too much radiation, they become ill or die. So radioactive substances must be handled very carefully. People who work in nuclear power stations wear special clothes to protect them from the radiation.

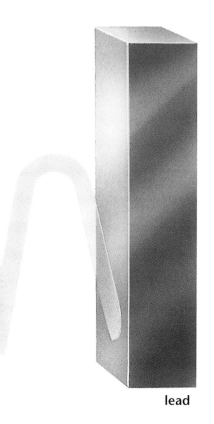

lead

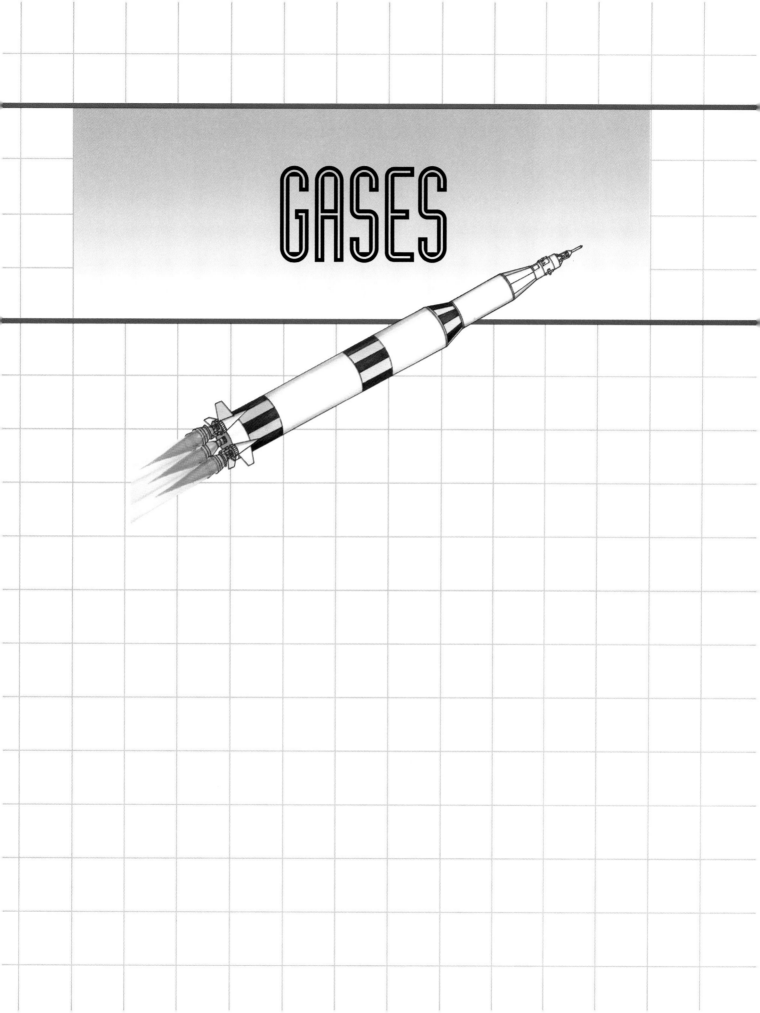

GASES

What are gases?

Have you ever wondered what everything in the world is made from? The answer is **matter**. Matter is anything that takes up space and has **inertia**. Inertia is the tendency of a motionless object to stay motionless, and of a moving object to keep moving at the same speed and in the same direction. The amount of matter in an object is called its **mass.**

There are millions of different things in the world, but there are just three main forms of matter. These are **solids, liquids,** and **gases.** Everything in the world belongs to one of these three main forms.

You can probably think of hundreds of different solids and liquids. Solids like stone and wood are hard and stay the same shape. Liquids like water and gasoline can flow from place to place. But gases are different.

How do we use gases?

Did you know that the air around you is a mixture of gases? Like most gases, those in clean air cannot be seen or smelled, and it is very difficult to make them stay in one place. You can place a solid in an open box, or a liquid in a cup, and it will stay there. But gases must be kept in completely closed containers or they will escape.

There are many different kinds of gas. Some are very useful. Oxygen is an important gas. It is found in the air. It helps humans and animals to stay alive, and fires to burn. Some gases come from under the ground. They are used as fuels and are burned for heating and cooking. One kind of gas helps balloons to float up in the air. Other gases help divers to breathe deep down in the sea.

Gases are also used in factories to make other useful substances such as plastics, bleach, and medicines. They are used in the manufacture of fertilizers, explosives, and dyes.

Natural gas is burning at this gas treatment plant in the shadow of Mount Egmont, New Zealand.

Find out more by looking
at pages **68–69**
72–73

Watching air

If you go out on a windy day, you can feel the wind tugging at your body, hair, and clothes. You can see the trees and flowers bending and the clouds racing across the sky. Perhaps an old newspaper is blown along the road, or the smoke from a chimney is blowing out sideways instead of going straight up.

What is doing all this pushing and shoving? What is moving everything around? It is **air.**

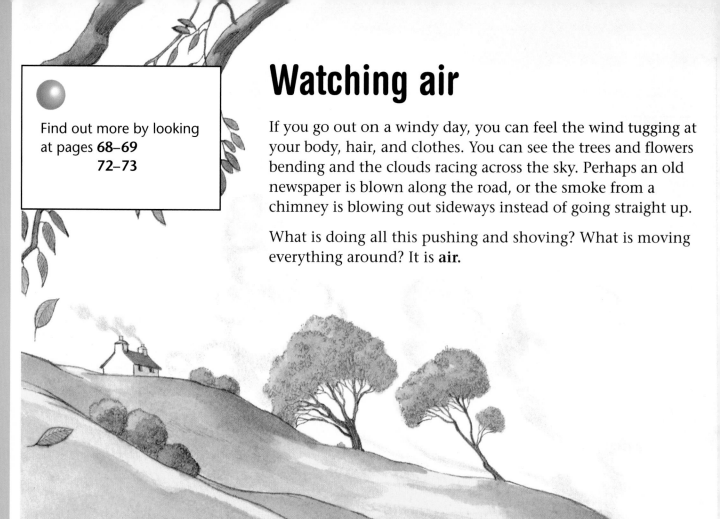

You will need:

a drinking glass or glass jar

a bowl of water

1. Fill the bowl with water. Hold the glass upside down above the water and push it slowly into the water. It is difficult to push it down because the air in it is lighter than water.

2. Now hold the glass, still upside down, on the bottom of the bowl. The water hasn't been able to get into the glass because it is still full of air. You can "see" the air inside.

You can see air

Here is an experiment that will let you "see" air.

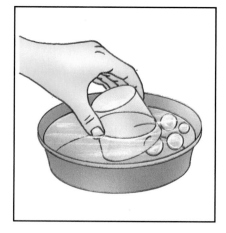

3. Tilt the glass. You will see bubbles of air coming to the surface of the water.

Air pushes upward

Air pushes from all sides on everyone and everything. It even pushes upward. You can show this by doing the following experiment.

You will need:

water

a drinking glass or glass jar

a piece of stiff cardboard

If the cardboard is too soft, or if the glass isn't completely full, this experiment will not work. You will spill the water. Do this experiment over a bathtub or sink, or outside.

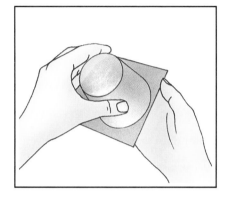

1. Fill the glass right to the top with water. Put the cardboard flat over the mouth of the glass.

2. Hold the cardboard firmly in place and carefully but quickly turn the glass upside down.

3. Take your hand away from the cardboard. It will stay in place and hold the water in the container. The air below the cardboard is pushing against it hard enough to keep the cardboard in place.

Find out more by looking at pages **78–79**
96–97

What's in the air?

About one-fifth of the air is oxygen. Human beings and other animals would not be able to survive without oxygen. When we breathe, our lungs take the oxygen we need from the air. Another very important gas in the air is carbon dioxide. When we breathe out, we release carbon dioxide into the air. Plants take in the carbon dioxide they need to live and grow, and they make oxygen. They then release the oxygen back into the air.

About four-fifths of the air is nitrogen. We breathe in nitrogen, but we don't use it. There are also small amounts of other gases in the air. Argon is one of these. We breathe in argon but, like nitrogen, we don't use it. The air also contains tiny amounts of water vapor.

*Green plants take in carbon dioxide from the air. Plants use carbon dioxide and water to make **glucose**, a type of sugar used for food energy. In the process, plants give out oxygen through their leaves.*

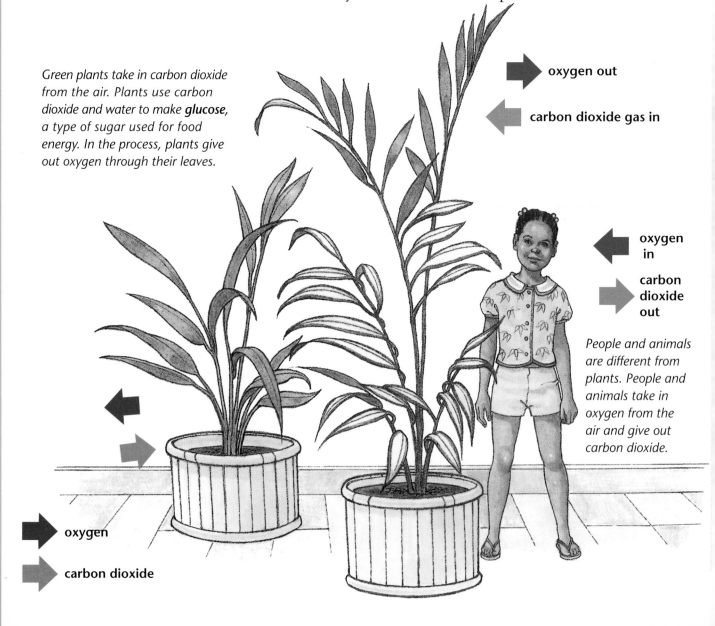

oxygen out

carbon dioxide gas in

oxygen in

carbon dioxide out

People and animals are different from plants. People and animals take in oxygen from the air and give out carbon dioxide.

oxygen

carbon dioxide

Using up oxygen

It isn't just living things that use the oxygen in the air. A fire needs oxygen to burn. There's no oxygen in outer space, so you can't light a match there.

Oxygen mixes with other substances too, and it sometimes changes them. Oxygen and water make iron turn to rust. As the iron rusts, it uses up oxygen in the air.

The rusting process needs oxygen

You will need:

soap

water

a shallow dish

food coloring

a felt-tipped pen

a nail or large pin

a ball of steel wool

a plastic cup

a large glass jar

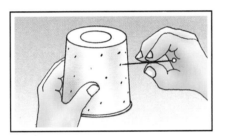

3. Use the nail or pin to prick the plastic cup in several places. Place the cup upside down in the water.

5. Leave your experiment for a few days. Add more water if necessary. Now and then, gently rock the jar to allow more water underneath. Be careful not to let in more air.

As time goes on, the steel wool will begin to rust. The rusting process uses up oxygen. As the air is used, the water level in the jar will rise to fill the space. Eventually, all the oxygen will have been used up and the water will take up about one-fifth of the air space in the jar.

1. Wash the steel wool in soapy water to remove any grease.

2. Pour about 1 inch (2.5 centimeters) of water into the dish. Put about six drops of food coloring in the water, and mix thoroughly.

4. Place the steel wool on top of the cup. Put the jar over the steel wool and the cup. Mark the water level on the side of the jar.

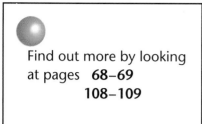

Find out more by looking
at pages **68–69**
      108–109

The atmosphere

Do you realize that we live at the bottom of an ocean of gas? This ocean of gas is called the **atmosphere**, and it completely surrounds Earth. The atmosphere extends from Earth's surface to about 1,000 miles (1,600 km) into space. We can best survive in the lower layers of the atmosphere at or near Earth's surface. This is because there is less and less air to breathe the farther you travel away from Earth's surface.

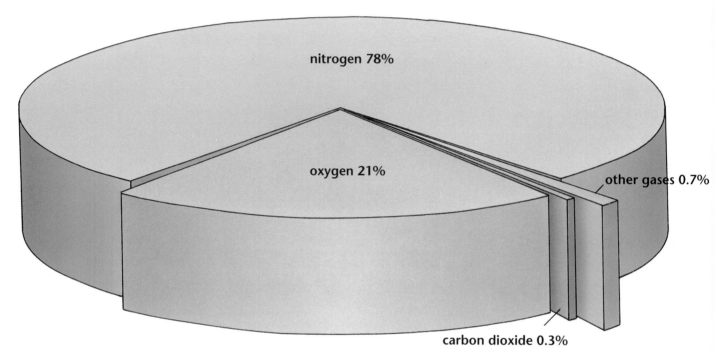

The air in the troposphere contains this mixture of gases.

The ozone layer

The atmosphere becomes thinner as its **altitude** (height) above Earth increases. In the **troposphere** are all the gases needed by living things on Earth. The next layer, the **stratosphere**, contains most of the **ozone layer.**

Ozone is a gas formed when ultraviolet rays from the sun change some of the oxygen in the atmosphere to ozone. Ozone makes a thin layer around Earth and blocks most of the sun's harmful ultraviolet rays, preventing them from reaching Earth. Some people think ozone smells like garlic. Others say it smells like seaweed. Oxygen has no smell at all. The temperature in the lower stratosphere is only about −67 °F (−55 °C).

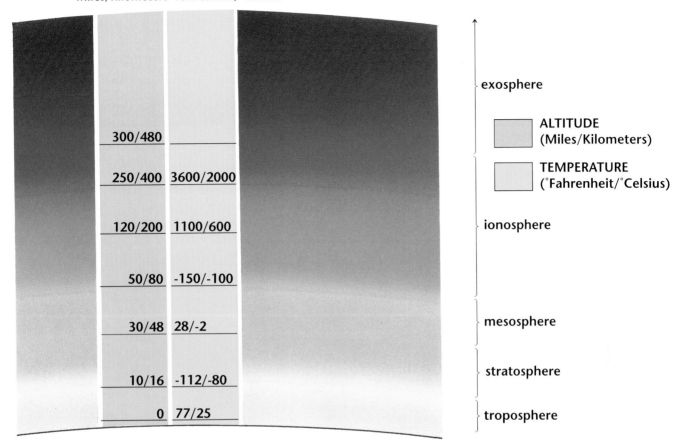

ALTITUDE TEMPERATURE
Miles/Kilometers °Fahrenheit/°Celsius

exosphere

ALTITUDE
(Miles/Kilometers)

TEMPERATURE
(°Fahrenheit/°Celsius)

ionosphere

mesosphere

stratosphere

troposphere

300/480

250/400   3600/2000

120/200   1100/600

50/80   -150/-100

30/48   28/-2

10/16   -112/-80

0   77/25

Beyond the troposphere

The stratosphere is about 20 miles (32 kilometers) thick. The temperature rises steadily as you pass through the stratosphere. But at the top, the temperature is still only 28 °F (−2 °C).

Above the stratosphere lies the **mesosphere**, and then the **thermosphere.** The lower part of the thermosphere and the upper part of the mesosphere are called the **ionosphere.** In this band of gases, the temperature becomes very hot. Radio messages can be sent over long distances by bouncing them off the ionosphere. Heavier gases like nitrogen tend to stay close to Earth. So above 60 miles (100 kilometers), you would find more of the lighter gases such as helium and hydrogen.

If you traveled more than 250 miles (400 kilometers) up, you would find so little air that satellites orbiting Earth in this region encounter almost no air resistance. The temperature is extremely hot—as much as 3600 °F (2000 °C). In the uppermost part of the atmosphere, the **exosphere**, Earth's atmosphere gradually merges into outer space.

The wind

We cannot see the **wind**, or moving air, but we can feel it and see what it does. A strong wind can damage buildings and uproot trees, but it can also turn the sails of a windmill. So we can use the wind to help us.

The power produced by the spinning sails of a windmill turns millstones to grind wheat. Many years ago, most wheat was ground in this way. Today, windmills can be used to turn machines called **generators.** Generators produce electricity.

You will need:

a pencil

a ruler

a piece of thin cardboard, 4 in. × 4 in. (10 cm × 10 cm)

a pin

scissors

a small bead

a stick, about 10 in. long (25 cm)

a small nail

Make a pinwheel

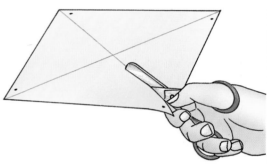

1. Draw two pencil lines, one from each corner of the card to the opposite corner. Make one small pinhole in each corner, just beside the line, and one hole in the center where the lines cross.

2. Cut along each pencil line toward the center. Cut halfway along each line.

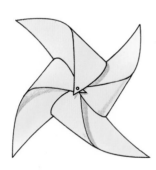

3. Bend over each corner so that all four corner holes are on top of the center hole. Push the pin through the holes.

4. Thread the bead onto the pin between the pinwheel and the stick. Push the point of the pin firmly into the stick. (You can use a small nail to start the hole before pushing the point of the pin into the stick.)

5. Now blow on your pinwheel. Which way does it turn? Does it work better if you blow from the front or from the side?

How strong is the wind?

Sometimes we need to know if there is going to be a strong wind. The speed of the wind is measured in miles (kilometers) per hour. Weather forecasters can tell us the strength of the wind by using the **Beaufort scale.** This scale describes what happens to buildings, trees, and water in the wind.

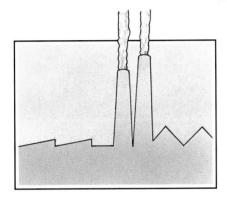

When the Beaufort scale is at 0, there is no wind at all. Smoke rises straight up into the air.

When the wind strength is 4–5 on the Beaufort scale, small trees and bushes bend in the wind.

The wind is quite strong when it measures 6–7 on the Beaufort scale, and large trees bend over.

Numbers 9–10 on the Beaufort scale mean gales. Trees may fall and tiles are blown off roofs.

Hurricanes and tornadoes are very violent storms. They read 12–17 on the Beaufort scale. The winds can blow at speeds of more than 74 miles (117 kilometers) per hour. Hurricanes and tornadoes can destroy anything in their paths.

Flying by gas

In 1783, the first person ever to fly went up in the air in a **hot-air balloon.** He was a Frenchman called Jean de Rozier. The first airplane flight wasn't made for another 120 years.

Balloons are still used for flying today. You may have seen a group of brightly colored hot-air balloons with baskets beneath them to carry passengers. The balloons rise upward because the gas inside them, such as helium, is lighter than air. Balloons are designed to rise and float in the air.

This hot-air balloon is rising up in front of the eastern Sierra Nevada in California.

Small balloons

The first balloons had a fire fixed underneath them, which filled the balloon with hot air. Today, balloonists fix burners to their balloons. The burners are connected to propane tanks and heat the air in the balloon when it gets too cold.

When you blow up a balloon, the air inside the balloon is not much warmer than the air outside, so the balloon doesn't sail off on its own. At fairs and parks, you can sometimes buy balloons filled with helium. These sail off by themselves, because the gas helium is lighter than the mixture of gases in the air. Balloons filled with helium can travel for long distances.

Find out more by looking at pages **76–77**

Airships use much less fuel than airplanes, but they travel much more slowly.

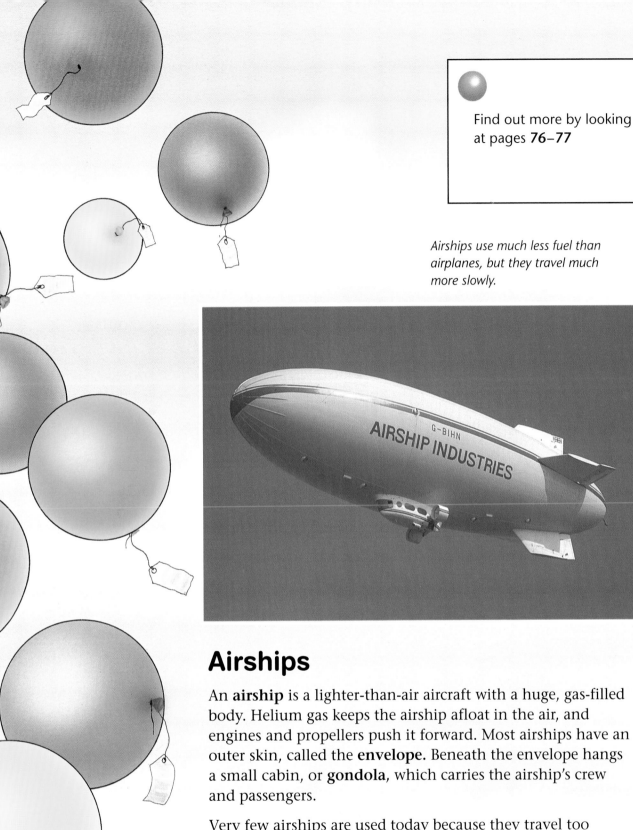

Airships

An **airship** is a lighter-than-air aircraft with a huge, gas-filled body. Helium gas keeps the airship afloat in the air, and engines and propellers push it forward. Most airships have an outer skin, called the **envelope**. Beneath the envelope hangs a small cabin, or **gondola**, which carries the airship's crew and passengers.

Very few airships are used today because they travel too slowly. The fastest ones reached speeds of only 80 miles (130 kilometers) per hour. Supersonic planes can now travel at speeds of over 1,200 miles (2,000 kilometers) per hour.

Find out more by looking at pages **74–75**

Airfoils

Balloons and airships stay up off the ground because the gas inside them is lighter, or less dense, than the air outside. But airplanes are heavier than air. How can they stay in the air?

What is an airfoil?

The shape of an airplane's wings gives it upward movement, or **lift.** If you look at an airplane from the side, you'll see that the upper surface of the wing is curved, and the lower surface is straighter. This shape of wing is called an **airfoil.**

When the plane is in flight, the air that passes over the top of the airfoil has to travel faster than the air that passes underneath it. This makes the air on the top push down on the airfoil less than the air pushing up from underneath. Therefore, the airplane is lifted up and stays in the air.

Take-off and landing

When an airplane is taking off, it needs a great deal of lift. If you look at a large airliner, you can see some movable **flaps** at the inside of the rear, or trailing, edge of the wings. These flaps can be lowered. When they are lowered, the flaps increase the top surface of the wing. As a result, air travels even farther over the top surface than over the bottom. The lowered flaps increase the lift force during take-off. During flight, the flaps are usually in a normal position, neither up nor down. But when the aircraft is landing, the flaps are lowered again.

Besides maintaining lift with reducing speeds, the lowered flaps help to slow the plane down.

When an airfoil moves through the air, it produces lift because the force of the air pushing down on its top surface is less than the force of the air from below. The uneven pressure causes lift.

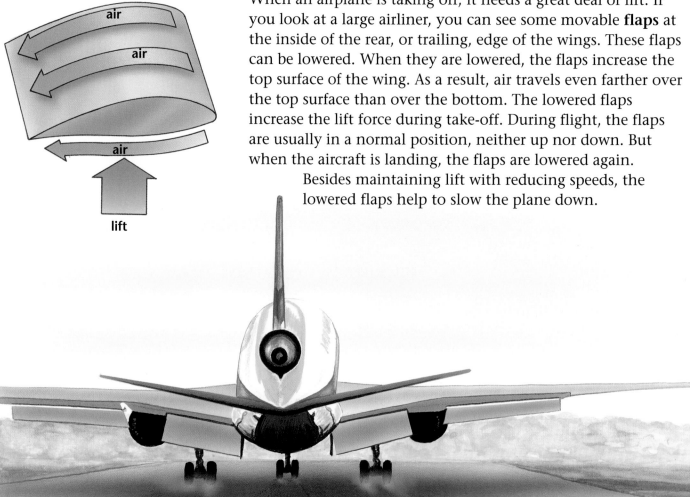

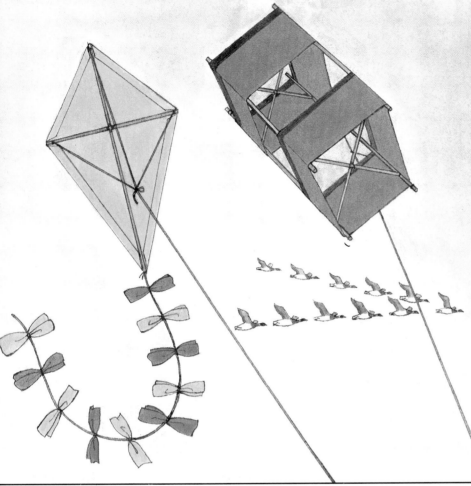

There are hundreds of different types of kites. When a kite is held at the correct angle, wind provides the lift to keep it in the air.

Making an airfoil

You will need:

a small sheet of paper

adhesive tape

1. Fold the paper in half. Move the edge of the upper half of the paper back a little from the edge of the lower half. It will bow upward. Carefully stick the edge down with adhesive tape.

2. You have made an airfoil. Put your airfoil on the edge of a table. Now place your mouth level with the edge of the table, and blow. What happens? Why?

What is density?

Helium gas is very light. It is lighter than air. But "lighter" isn't really the right word to use here. Scientists say that helium is less **dense** than air because it weighs less than the same amount, or volume, of air. Another way of describing helium is to say that it has a lower **density** than air. Carbon dioxide is more dense than air, so we say it has a higher density than air.

One way of understanding density is to imagine three boxes, all the same size. One box is full of air, one is full of helium, and one is full of carbon dioxide. If you weighed the boxes, the one containing carbon dioxide would weigh the most and the one containing helium would weigh the least.

There would be the same volume of gas in each box, but their different densities would make them have different weights.

Gases all have different densities. Some gases, such as helium, are lighter than air. Others, such as carbon dioxide, are heavier than air. These boxes of gas all contain the same volume. They are being weighed on scales that measure very small amounts.

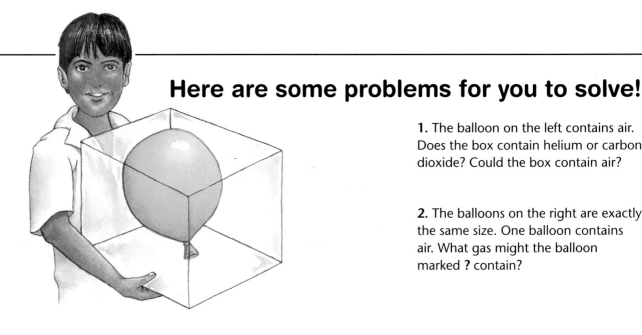

Here are some problems for you to solve!

1. The balloon on the left contains air. Does the box contain helium or carbon dioxide? Could the box contain air?

2. The balloons on the right are exactly the same size. One balloon contains air. What gas might the balloon marked **?** contain?

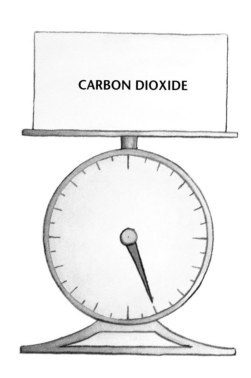

AIR

CARBON DIOXIDE

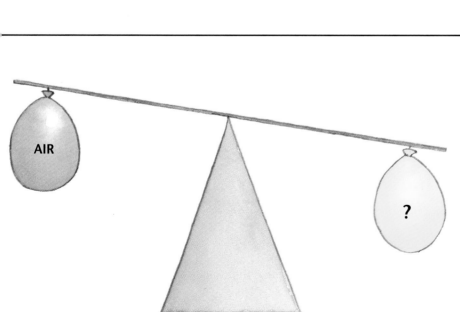

AIR

?

Answers

1. The box contains carbon dioxide. The balloon is floating, so the box must contain a gas that is more dense than the gas in the balloon. If the box contained air, the balloon would not rise.

2. The answer is carbon dioxide. The lower balloon is the heavier one, so it must contain a gas that is more dense than air.

Find out more by looking at pages **66–67**

What is air pressure?

Look out of your window. Is the air moving? It is probably moving enough to make branches sway. The weight of this air pressing down all around Earth produces **air pressure.** If you live high up above sea level, or if you go to the top of a skyscraper, the air pressure is less. This is because there is less air above you, therefore less air pressure.

On Earth's surface, or near it, air always moves from areas of **high pressure** to areas of **low pressure.** Temperature has a great effect on air pressure. As warm air rises, it produces an area of low pressure near the ground. Wind is produced when cooler, heavier air flows toward the low pressure area, replacing the rising air. As the air pressure changes from place to place, and from day to day, it helps move air across Earth's surface all the time.

Cool air is heavier than warm air. Cool air sinks down from an area of high pressure, while warm air rises, creating an area of low pressure.

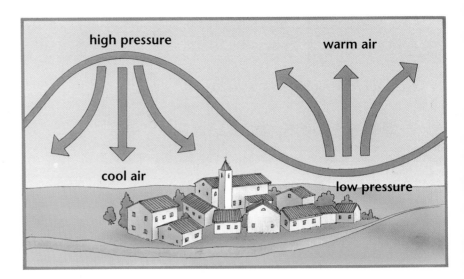

How do barometers work?

You can forecast what the weather will be like for the next few hours by measuring the air pressure.

The instrument used to measure changes in air pressure is called a **barometer.** If you have one at home, it is probably an **aneroid barometer.** There's a needle behind a glass-covered dial marked "Fine," "Fair," and "Stormy." If you tap the glass lightly in the morning, the needle points to the weather you can expect that day.

Types of barometers

Inside the aneroid barometer is a metal box, or chamber, from which almost all the air has been removed. The metal of the chamber is so thin that small changes in the air pressure outside it make the metal bend. This makes the needle turn around and point to a new position on the dial.

A **mercury barometer** measures the air pressure more accurately. A long glass tube is filled with **mercury**, a silvery liquid metal. The tube is sealed at one end and placed open end down in a small dish of mercury. Some of the mercury stays in the tube. It is held there by the air pressure at the surface of the mercury in the dish. As the air pressure changes, the column of mercury moves up or down. A scale beside the tube shows the pressure measurements.

The aneroid barometer contains a small metal chamber that is sensitive to changes in air pressure.

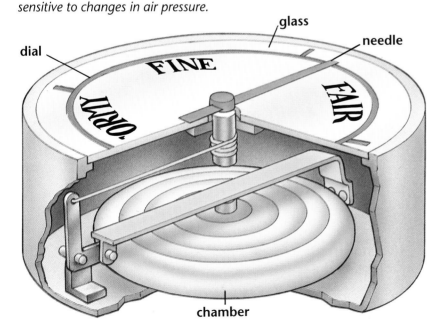

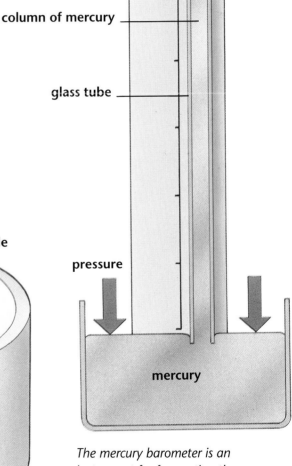

The mercury barometer is an instrument for forecasting the weather.

Find out more by looking at pages **100–101**

Rockets

Blow up a balloon and then let it go. The force of the high-pressure air coming out of the neck makes the balloon rush aimlessly in all directions. This type of force pushing the balloon forwards is called **thrust.** It is the same force that makes rockets move.

Space rockets and fireworks rockets all use hot gases to produce thrust. A mixture of substances is set on fire so that it burns very rapidly. The force created by this burning is channeled in one direction, and the thrust makes the rocket move off in the opposite direction.

Controlling the thrust

You can stop a balloon from flying out of control.

You will need:

a balloon

a medium-sized button

Make sure the balloon end with the button is not pointing toward your eyes.

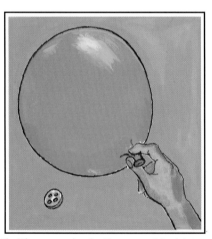

1. Blow up the balloon and hold it by the neck. Do not tie a knot in the end.

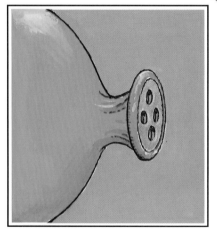

2. Slip the button into the balloon's neck so that the neck closes tightly about the button.

3. Let the balloon go. It will fly off in a fairly direct line. It will take quite a long time for the balloon to empty, because the air inside cannot escape very quickly.

The stretched rubber of the balloon puts pressure on the air inside, but the button openings control the thrust.

Producing thrust

Various mixtures of substances can be used to make thrust. A mixture of the two gases hydrogen and oxygen is often used for space rockets. These gases are cooled and turned into liquids. As liquids, they can be stored in a smaller space than in their normal state.

When hydrogen is mixed with oxygen, the smallest spark can make this mixture burst into flames. The hot gases catch fire inside the rocket and shoot out from the bottom of the rocket. The force of this fire can be controlled and channeled to give the rocket the thrust it needs to take it into orbit around Earth or into outer space.

The space shuttle Discovery takes off from the Kennedy Space Center, Florida. Hot gases create the thrust that launches the rocket into space.

84

Find out more by looking at pages **106–107**

Hot and cold gases

What happens when water boils in a pan? If you don't take the pan away from the heat, all the water will boil away as a gas, or **vapor.** This change from liquid into vapor is called **evaporation.** A substance can be a solid, a liquid, or a gas. We usually see water as a liquid. When water is very cold, it becomes solid ice. When it is very hot, it becomes a gas. The state of a substance depends on its temperature.

Carbon dioxide gas becomes a solid at very low temperatures. This solid is called **dry ice.** At room temperature, dry ice will turn back into a gas. It is used in motion pictures and on stage at rock concerts to produce swirling clouds of mist. But one of its main uses is for food storage.

Altering pressure

Another way of changing the state of a substance is to change the force pressing down on it. This force is called **pressure.** Imagine opening a bottle of water in outer space where there is almost no pressure. The water would evaporate at once!

When carbon dioxide gas is kept at a very low temperature, it turns into a solid called dry ice. The dry ice turns back into a gas at room temperature.

Gases expand and contract

All gases are made up of tiny particles called **atoms**. These atoms are always moving. Groups of atoms are called **molecules**. When a gas is heated, its molecules move about faster, bouncing off one another. As the molecules become scattered, the gas takes up more space. It **expands** (spreads out) and becomes less dense. When a gas cools, it takes up less space, or **contracts**. This experiment shows how air contracts when it is cooled.

You will need:

a sausage-shaped balloon   a refrigerator or freezer

cotton thread

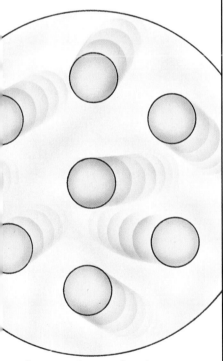

slow-moving molecules

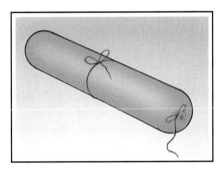

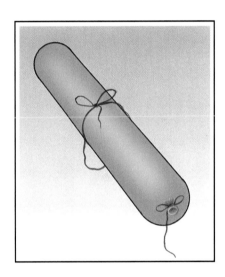

1. Blow up the balloon and tie the end. Tie a piece of thread around the balloon, just tightly enough so that the thread doesn't move.

3. Take out the balloon. Feel how the balloon is different. Explain what has happened, and why.

As the air in the balloon warms up, the balloon changes. How? Explain.

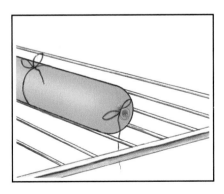

2. Put the balloon in a refrigerator or freezer overnight or longer.

fast-moving molecules

When a gas is heated, the gas molecules move about more quickly and take up more space, or expand.

Find out more by looking
at pages **84–85**
88–89

Gases under pressure

One of the most important properties of gases is that they can be squeezed, or **compressed**, into a smaller space. You can discover this for yourself.

You will need:

water

a plastic bottle with a top

Squeezing the air

Do you think it is easier to compress air or water? Find out the answer by doing this simple experiment.

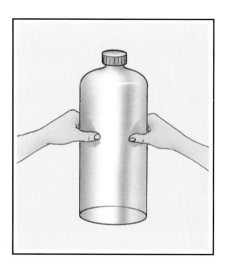

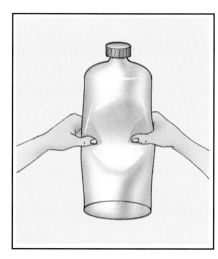

1. Fill the bottle with water and screw on the top. Then squeeze the sides of the bottle. How does water respond to pressure?

2. Empty out the water and screw on the top. Squeeze the sides of the bottle again. Does air respond to pressure in the same way as water?

Using compressed gas

We use compressed gases in many different ways. You have probably seen workers digging up a road with drills powered by compressed air. There may be a stove or heater at home or at school that burns compressed gas. The gas is stored in metal containers and is often called **bottled gas.** Butane and propane are two kinds of bottled gas. The high pressure in the container keeps propane in its liquid form.

Bottled gas

This gas bottle contains a liquid that changes into a gas when it is released.

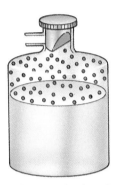

1. The valve on the bottle is closed. Gas is filling the space above the liquid.

2. The valve is opened and some gas is let out. The pressure inside the bottle is reduced and some more liquid changes into gas.

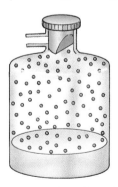

3. The valve is closed again, but now there is more gas and less liquid inside the bottle.

How a pump works

When you pump up your bicycle tires or a football, you are making use of compressed air. Inside a bicycle pump is a small device called a **valve.** A valve allows a gas or a liquid to pass through it in one direction only. Attached to the tire is another valve.

When the plunger of the pump is pushed down, the valve attached to the tire opens and air is forced into the tire. As the plunger is pulled back, the valve on the tire closes so that no air can escape.

At the same time, the valve on the end of the plunger allows more air into the pump. Next time the plunger is pushed down, this air is forced into the tire.

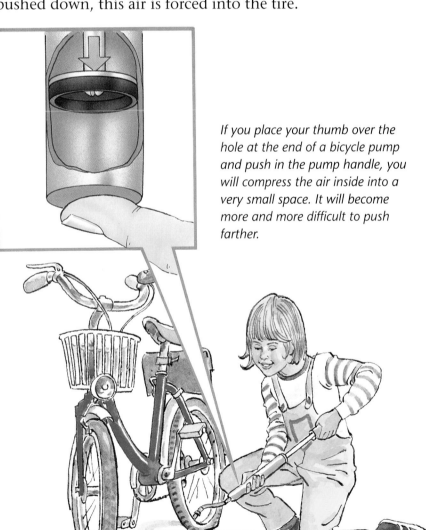

If you place your thumb over the hole at the end of a bicycle pump and push in the pump handle, you will compress the air inside into a very small space. It will become more and more difficult to push farther.

Find out more by looking at pages **86–87**

Gases in liquids

Pour a teaspoonful of salt into a glass of water. Now stir it and watch the salt slowly disappear from sight. It is **dissolving** in the water. How do you know the salt is still there? Try tasting a drop of the water.

Gases also dissolve in liquids. There is a great deal of dissolved oxygen in both salt water and fresh water. Fish take in water and extract the oxygen from it. This is how they breathe.

Bubbles of gas

Every time you have a carbonated drink, you are drinking gas that has been dissolved in liquid. This gas is carbon dioxide. Pressure is used to make carbon dioxide dissolve.

The carbonated drink is still under pressure when it is canned in a factory. When you open a can containing a carbonated drink, you release the pressure and thousands of bubbles of carbon dioxide stream to the surface. As you drink, you can feel some of the bubbles popping on your tongue.

Shake your drink!

If you shake the can before opening it, you will affect the carbonation in the drink. Shaking the drink makes more tiny bubbles of gas form. When the can is opened, the gas in these bubbles expands instantly, making the drink froth and foam.

If you leave the can open, the carbonation will eventually disappear. Because it is no longer under pressure, the carbon dioxide will escape into the atmosphere.

Making bubbles

Try producing bubbles of gas in a liquid for yourself.

You will need:

a teaspoon

baking powder

a glass

water

Put half a teaspoonful of baking powder into a glass and add water. Stir the mixture. Describe what happens as the baking powder dissolves.

To show that there is air dissolved in water, fill a glass with tap water and leave it for several hours. What has happened inside the glass?

Find out more by looking
at pages **68–69**
         88–89

Handling gases

If you wanted to bring some air from outside into your house, it would be quite easy. You could take an empty jar, wave it around outside until all the indoor air had gone, and then put the lid back on and go indoors.

Gas over water

Putting other gases into containers is more difficult than collecting fresh air in a jar. There is a way of doing it described as **collecting gas over water.** This process is used a great deal in science and industry for gases that do not dissolve in water.

In research laboratories, scientists often need to find out what a substance is made of. They might heat the substance to see if a gas is produced. One way to collect that gas is by bubbling it through an inverted water-filled jar. The collection is complete when the jar has been emptied of water and is full of gas. The gas collected in this way should be pure and have no air mixed with it. Scientists can then run tests on the pure gas.

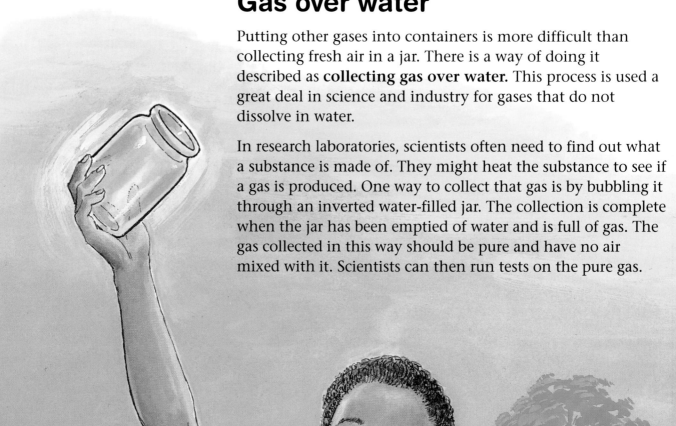

Collecting your breath

You can collect your breath underwater very easily.

You will need:

water

a bendable drinking straw

a plastic bowl or basin

a jar with a tight-fitting lid

1. Place the jar in the bowl or basin. Pour enough water into the bowl to cover and fill the jar completely.

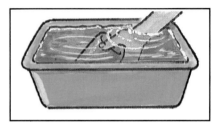

2. Turn the jar upside down without lifting the neck above the water's surface. The jar will stay full of water.

3. Tip the jar slightly to one side and hold it firmly in one hand. Put one end of the straw directly under the mouth of the jar and the other end in your mouth.

4. Blow gently through the straw. Your breath will slowly take the place of the water inside the jar. Keep on blowing until nearly all the water has disappeared from the jar.

5. The jar will now be almost completely filled with your breath. Working underwater, screw or push the lid on the jar.

Because your breath is full of carbon dioxide, you will now have a jar with more carbon dioxide in it than there is in normal air.

Find out more by looking at pages **68–69**

Breathing

Have you ever tried to stop breathing? Sometimes we hold our breath when we are trying to listen to a faint sound. But we soon have to start breathing again. We breathe all the time, whether awake or asleep, without even thinking about it. Our breathing system is automatic.

There is a mixture of gases, including oxygen, in the air. Because our bodies need and use that oxygen, we breathe it in, or **inhale** it. Other gases in the air aren't of any use to us. We breathe them out, or **exhale** them.

When we are in a room with a lot of other people and the windows are closed, we may start to feel sleepy. This is because many people are using up the oxygen in the air and breathing out carbon dioxide. There is less and less oxygen to help us produce energy. As soon as we open a window and let in some more oxygen, we start to feel less tired.

Athletes, like this runner, need plenty of oxygen to help them move. They need to breathe quickly, deeply, and often.

You will need:

a friend to keep the score

a notebook and pencil

a watch with a second hand

Test your breathing rate

Depending on what you are doing, you breathe more quickly or more slowly. The speed at which you breathe is called your **breathing rate.** When you're asleep, you don't need much energy. You need less oxygen, and so you breathe slowly. If you're running in a race, you need plenty of energy, so you breathe more quickly and deeply.

See how quickly or slowly you breathe when you are doing different activities.

1. Sit still in a chair for about five minutes, with your eyes closed. After this time, have your friend count how many breaths you take in one minute.

Use the watch to measure the time accurately. One inhalation and one exhalation count as one breath. Write down the result.

2. Repeat this counting process after running 200 feet (60 meters), riding your bicycle, running upstairs, and skipping 20 times. Leave a few minutes between each activity to allow your breathing to settle down.

Which activity made you breathe most quickly? When did you breathe most slowly?

Combustion

Sitting beside a coal or a log fire on a cold night is very cozy, isn't it? Next time you have a chance to do this, watch the flames dancing. The flames of a fire are usually red, orange, or yellow, but sometimes they are blue, green, or mauve.

The flames are made by the burning gases given off from the coal or wood as it gets hot. Another word for burning is **combustion.** There are many other examples of combustion in our homes. Look around and see how many you can write down.

Combustion takes place when the oxygen in the air combines with another gas, solid, or liquid to give off energy. This energy is given off in the form of heat, and usually light, too.

Slow combustion

When you have a barbecue, you burn charcoal. When it is hot, charcoal combines directly with the oxygen in the air and starts to glow. Charcoal doesn't give off gases first, so there are no flames in a charcoal fire. This kind of burning is called **slow combustion.**

Anything that burns can be dangerous. Never play with fire. Don't even strike a match unless an adult is with you.

*Materials need to be heated to a certain temperature before they burn. The lowest temperature at which an object begins to burn is called the **kindling temperature**, and it differs from one material to another.*

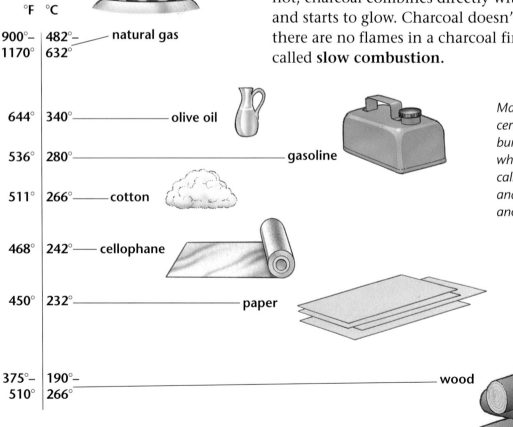

°F	°C	
900°–1170°	482°–632°	natural gas
644°	340°	olive oil
536°	280°	gasoline
511°	266°	cotton
468°	242°	cellophane
450°	232°	paper
375°–510°	190°–266°	wood

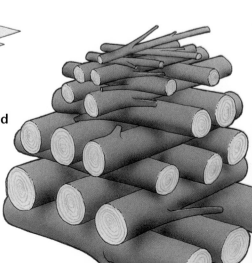

Fires need oxygen

Fires need oxygen to keep burning. To stop a fire, we must cut off the oxygen supply. When you blow out a candle, your breath cools the wick so that no more gas comes from the wax. To make sure that a match is out, you could bury it in sand. This prevents oxygen from reaching it.

People put out bigger fires with **fire extinguishers.** Some extinguishers use carbon dioxide to cut off the oxygen supply from a fire. Others smother the fire with foam or powder made from chemicals. Water will cut off the oxygen supply, too, as well as cooling the fire, but it isn't safe to use water on a fire involving electrical equipment or wiring.

Fire fighters in protective clothing spray foam onto a burning airplane.

Find out more by looking
at pages **88–89**
104–105

Putting air to work

There are four main gases in the air—**nitrogen, oxygen, argon,** and **carbon dioxide.** Nitrogen makes up about 78 percent of the air and oxygen about 21 percent. Argon, carbon dioxide, and other gases account for the remaining 1 percent. These gases are used in different ways.

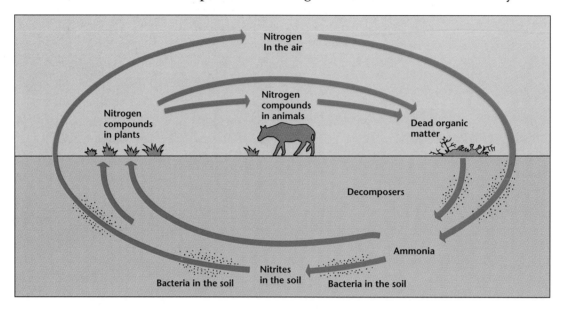

Nitrogen

Nitrogen isn't of much use on its own, but it combines with other chemicals in important ways. Our bodies need special food substances, called **proteins,** for growth and energy and for replacement of body cells. Proteins are partly made from atoms of nitrogen.

We cannot use nitrogen directly from the air. Instead, we must take it in from plants, which have absorbed it from the soil, or from the meat of animals that have eaten plants.

Nitrogen atoms can join up with oxygen atoms and the atoms of other chemicals to make substances called **nitrates.** Some nitrates are used in explosives. Others are used as fertilizers to help feed crops.

Oxygen

Oxygen is used with other gases to melt and join metals in a process called **welding.** It's also used in making steel. Liquid oxygen and liquid hydrogen are mixed together to make rocket fuel. Astronauts, deep-sea divers, and mountain climbers breathe in a mixture of oxygen and other gases from special air tanks they carry with them.

Argon

Argon doesn't join up easily with other substances. It is used as a gas to make some electric light bulbs shine. Sometimes argon is used during welding to prevent certain metals from catching fire. It keeps the air away from the welding flame.

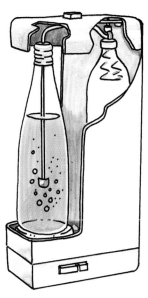

Carbon dioxide

Carbon dioxide is used in carbonated drinks and in fire extinguishers. Dry ice is carbon dioxide in its solid form. Plants use carbon dioxide from the air to make food.

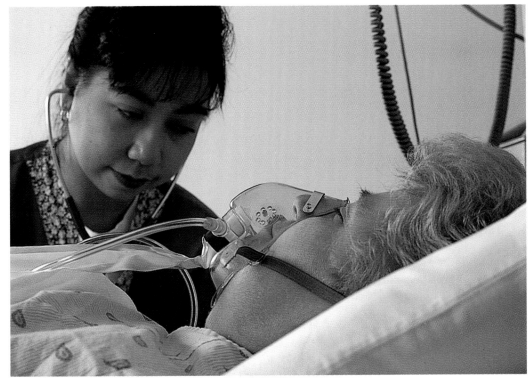

Oxygen is also used in hospitals. Patients with serious breathing problems can breathe air containing a large supply of oxygen through a special mask.

Find out more by looking at pages **86–87**
100–101

Separating air

The gases in the air can be used for different purposes. But first they have to be separated from each other. A process called **distillation** is used to separate oxygen from the other gases in the air.

Distilling liquids

Imagine running a bath of hot water on a cold day. Some of the hot water becomes water vapor and fills the bathroom with mist. When this mist touches the cold bathroom tiles or windows, it **condenses**. This means that it changes back into a liquid.

This liquid is pure water. It has been **distilled**, or separated out, from all the other substances dissolved in the tap water.

In order to obtain liquid oxygen from the air, the air has to be turned into a liquid. The different gases can then be separated by distillation.

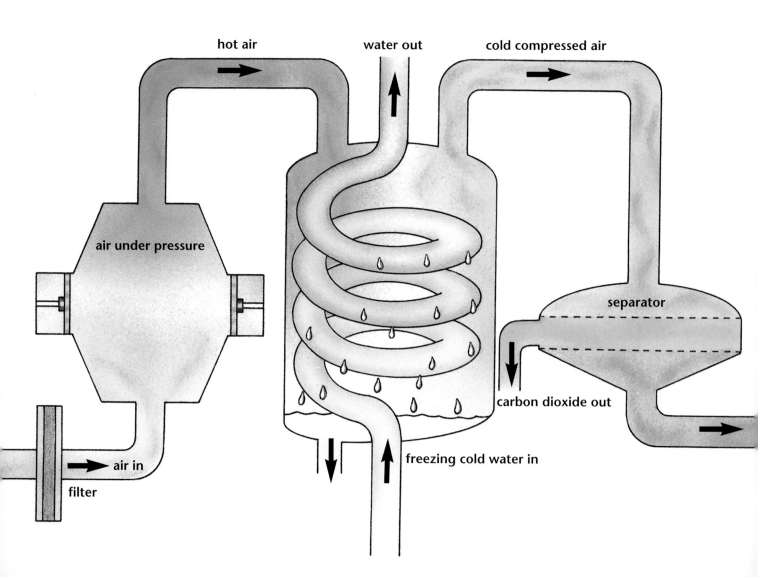

hot air   water out   cold compressed air

air under pressure

separator

carbon dioxide out

air in

filter

freezing cold water in

Distilling gases

Distilling gases is a process similar to distilling liquids, but with one important difference. Instead of using heat, we use cold.

Different gases change into a liquid or a solid state at different temperatures. If you make air colder, the first gas to change its state is carbon dioxide. It turns into dry ice at $-109.3\,°F$ ($-78.5\,°C$). Oxygen is the next to change. It becomes a liquid at about $-297\,°F$ ($-183\,°C$). Then argon changes to a liquid at $-302.3\,°F$ ($-185.7\,°C$). But to make liquid nitrogen, the temperature has to reach $-320.4\,°F$ ($-195.8\,°C$).

Another way of distilling air is to cool it until it becomes a liquid, and then to let the temperature rise slowly. As each gas evaporates at a different temperature, it is collected and stored in a sealed container.

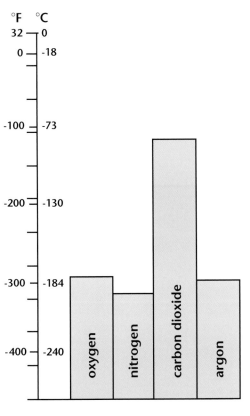

This chart shows the boiling point of the four main gases in the air. At its boiling point, a gas changes its state.

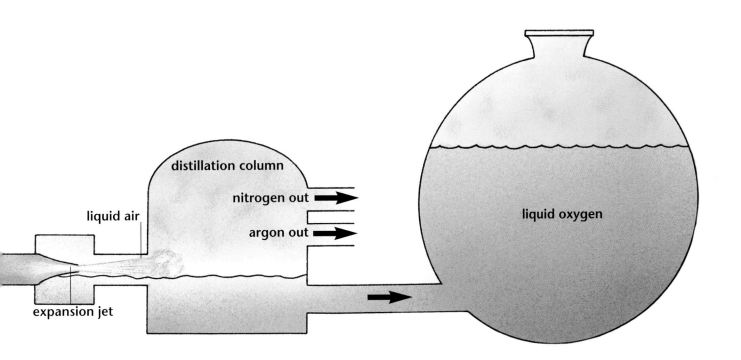

Gases as liquids

Gases can be cooled until they become liquids. Some gases don't become liquids until they reach very low temperatures.

Helium doesn't become liquid until it reaches a temperature of −452 °F (−268.9 °C). You can get some idea of how cold that is by comparing this temperature to the freezing point of water, 32 °F (0 °C)!

Do you remember what happens when gases are heated? Their molecules become more active, bouncing off each other and spreading out. The same thing happens to liquids when they are heated. There is more space between the molecules, and so the liquid can turn into a gas.

When a gas becomes a liquid, the opposite happens. As the gas is cooled, the molecules become less active and stay closer together. They take up less space. But it is quite difficult to turn gases into liquids, so why do people bother? There are several reasons.

heated gas

thermometer

cooled gas

When a gas is heated, its molecules move around more quickly. When a gas is cooled, its molecules come closer together, moving less and less. If cooled enough, the gas becomes a liquid.

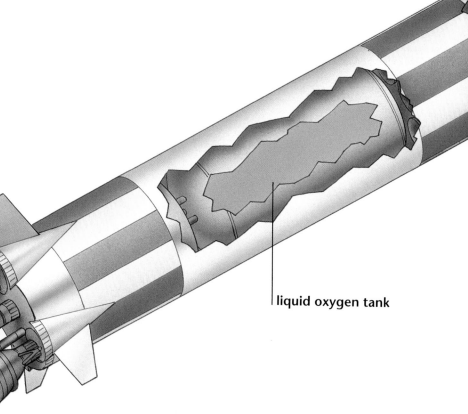

liquid oxygen tank

Find out more by looking
at pages **84–85**
86–87
98–99

Multistage rockets use liquid hydrogen and oxygen as fuel. The fuel is kept in tanks. When the fuel in a tank runs out, that section of the rocket drops away and engines in other sections of the rocket take over.

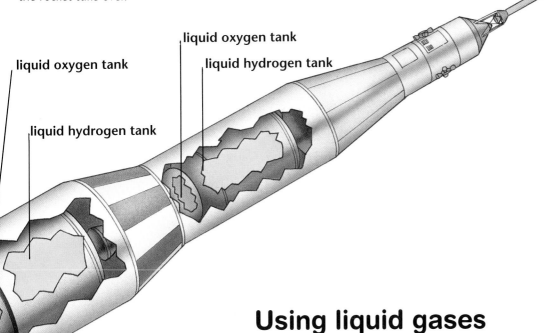

liquid oxygen tank

liquid oxygen tank

liquid hydrogen tank

liquid hydrogen tank

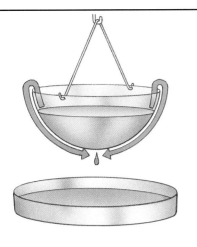

Superfluid helium doesn't flow like other liquids. It crawls over the sides of a container!

Using liquid gases

Some processes in industry need liquid gases. For example, in some large refrigerators, liquid nitrogen is used to cool the contents. Gases in liquid form are also easier to store and transport because they take up less space than they do in their gaseous form.

Gases as liquids are also easier to control. Liquid hydrogen and oxygen are used as fuel for space rockets. Their flow to the rocket motors can be controlled to produce just the right amount of thrust.

Scientists are interested in certain liquid gases because they behave in a very curious way. Liquid helium, for example, is a **superfluid.** It becomes a superfluid when chilled to an extremely low temperature. It doesn't follow the usual behavior of liquids. It is so fluid that it flows up and over the sides of its container.

Discoveries like this help scientists find out more about what matter is and how it behaves.

Taking your air with you

There is no air out in space or in the depths of the ocean, so astronauts and deep-sea divers have to take their own supply of air with them. Mountain climbers and aircraft crews flying at high altitude also have to take their own air, because they travel to places where the air is very thin.

Breathing oxygen

In order to live, we have to breathe oxygen. If we are going somewhere where there is little or no oxygen, we have to take our own supply with us.

The air we breathe in is a mixture of gases. So the oxygen in **breathing apparatus** usually has to be mixed with another gas to make it safe to breathe. The other gas is usually nitrogen, but sometimes it is helium.

Deep-sea divers and fire fighters use similar types of breathing apparatus. They carry tanks of compressed air on their backs.

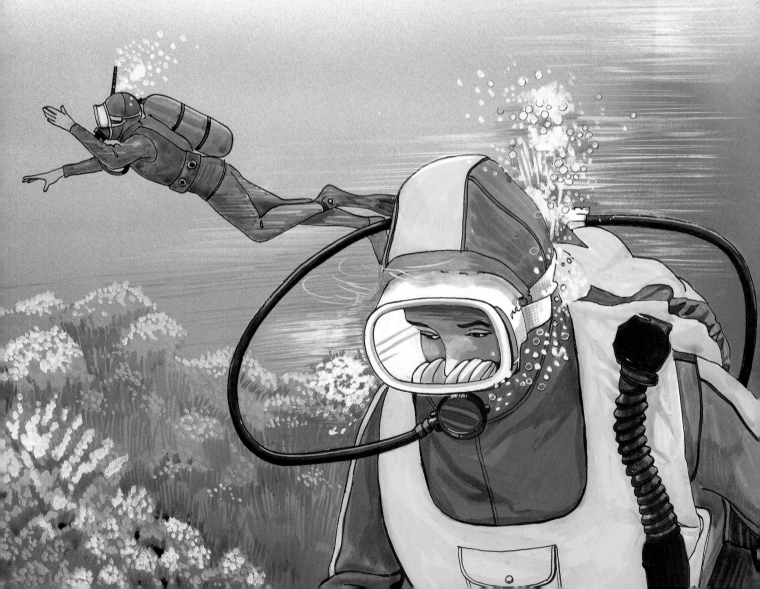

Breathing compressed air

Find out more by looking at pages **86–87**

The air supply that astronauts or divers take with them has to be compressed, otherwise they would be carrying huge gas tanks around with them.

Because the air is compressed, the diver breathes more molecules of air than normal. When the diver rises to the surface, the pressure from the water decreases, and the air he or she has breathed expands. The expanding air can damage or even kill the diver if he or she rises to the surface too quickly.

One type of breathing apparatus is called the **aqualung** or **scuba**. Using this, an experienced diver can go down 130 feet (40 meters) below the surface of the ocean.

Fire fighters also need breathing apparatus. Burning materials produce smoke and dangerous gases. They also remove oxygen from the air. Fire fighters carry tanks of compressed air and wear breathing apparatus similar to an aqualung.

Cutting and welding

Welding is a method of joining metals together in such a way that they **fuse**, or melt together, so they cannot be pulled or shaken apart.

When metals are welded together, two pieces of metal are heated to such a high temperature that their edges become liquid. Then, while they are in this state, the two pieces of metal are held together. When they cool down again, they will be stuck tightly to each other.

Using acetylene gas

Welders have to direct very intense heat onto a small space. If they want to join two edges of metal together, they need to heat only the edges.

One type of welding uses a jet of burning **acetylene gas** as its source of heat. Acetylene is made from hydrogen and carbon. It produces very great heat when it is burned with pure oxygen.

Welders use a tool called an **acetylene torch.** This can be adjusted to make a very hot, small fire that can be directed to just where it is needed.

Welders have to wear protective goggles when welding metals together. The sparks from the metal and the bright light can easily damage their eyes.

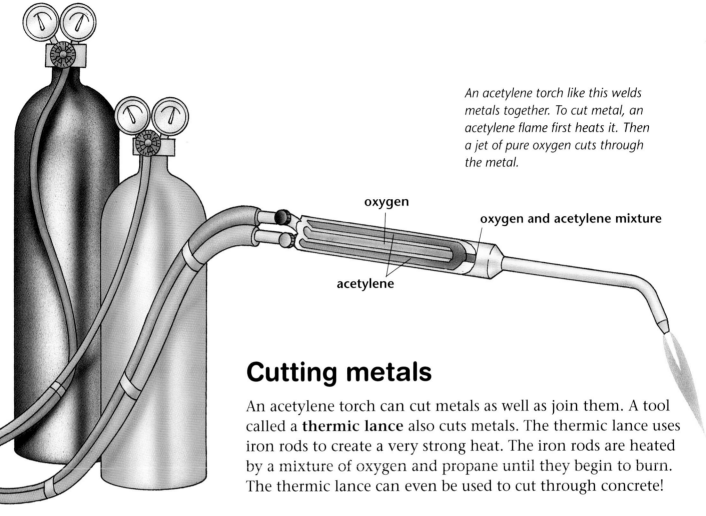

An acetylene torch like this welds metals together. To cut metal, an acetylene flame first heats it. Then a jet of pure oxygen cuts through the metal.

oxygen

oxygen and acetylene mixture

acetylene

Cutting metals

An acetylene torch can cut metals as well as join them. A tool called a **thermic lance** also cuts metals. The thermic lance uses iron rods to create a very strong heat. The iron rods are heated by a mixture of oxygen and propane until they begin to burn. The thermic lance can even be used to cut through concrete!

You will need:

two candles

an old knife with a plastic or wooden handle

Cutting the easy way

You can do an experiment to show how easily a thermic lance can cut through substances.

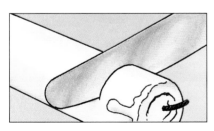

1. Put one candle on its side and cut through it with the knife. Notice how much pressure from your hand it takes to get through it.

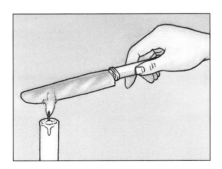

2. Ask an adult to light the other candle. Hold the knife blade in the flame for several minutes. **Don't touch the blade.**

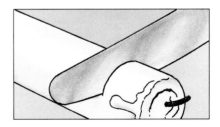

3. Put the candle you've already cut through on its side again. Rest the sharp edge of the knife blade on it. If it is hot enough, the blade will cut through the wax without any pressure from your hand.

Find out more by looking at pages **28–29** **84–85**

Water vapor

Have you ever woken up on a cold winter morning to find the window panes covered with patterns like leaves? These patterns are made by a thin layer of ice that has formed on the inside of the glass.

Ice formation

How did the ice get there? We think of water as a liquid, but it can also be a gas. There is water vapor mixed in with the gases we breathe out. The water vapor from our breath builds up in the air.

If it is colder outside than indoors, the window panes are cold. When the water vapor inside the house reaches this cold glass, the vapor cools and turns into liquid water. This change is called **condensation.** We have already seen that hot water condenses in a bathroom. But if the window panes are cold enough, the water will freeze to form a thin layer of ice.

The frost on this car has formed overnight. Water vapor condensed in the cold weather and changed into liquid water. This water froze and turned into ice.

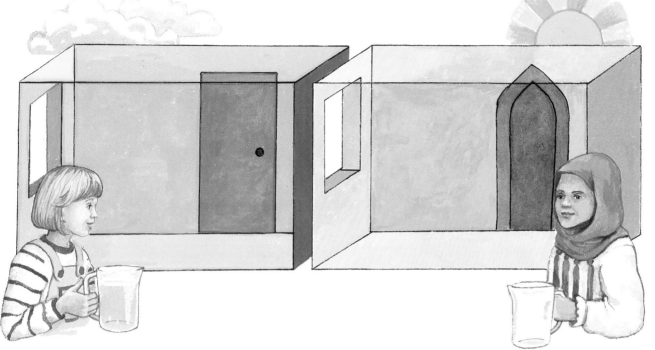

The full jug on the left represents how much water may be present in the air in a warm, damp climate. The jug on the right is empty, because in the hot, dry desert climate, there is almost no water in the air.

The humidity of the air

We use the word **humidity** to describe the amount of water vapor contained in the air. Hot air can hold a lot of water vapor. Cold air holds less. Next time you are outside on a cold day, watch your breath. You can see the water vapor in your breath condense into a cloud of tiny water droplets. You can see this happening on a hot day if you try this experiment.

You will need:

a glass tumbler

a refrigerator

2. Blow into the tumbler a few times. Describe what happens.

1. Leave the tumbler in the refrigerator overnight so that the glass gets really cold. Take it out the following morning.

Find out more by looking at pages **70–71** **84–85**

Gases in space

Oxygen is a very important gas for life on Earth. Animals have to breathe oxygen in order to live. But another important gas is hydrogen. Hydrogen makes up about three-quarters of all the matter in the universe.

Hydrogen atoms

An atom of hydrogen is the simplest type of atom. It has only two parts—one electron circling around one proton. But an oxygen atom has 24 parts—eight electrons circling around eight protons and eight neutrons.

Nearly all scientists think that when the universe first came into existence, it exploded in a great ball of fire. When this fire began to cool, hydrogen atoms were the first to be created. The fire also resulted in a small amount of helium. A helium atom is the next simplest type of atom after a hydrogen atom. This explanation of how the universe began is called the "big bang" theory.

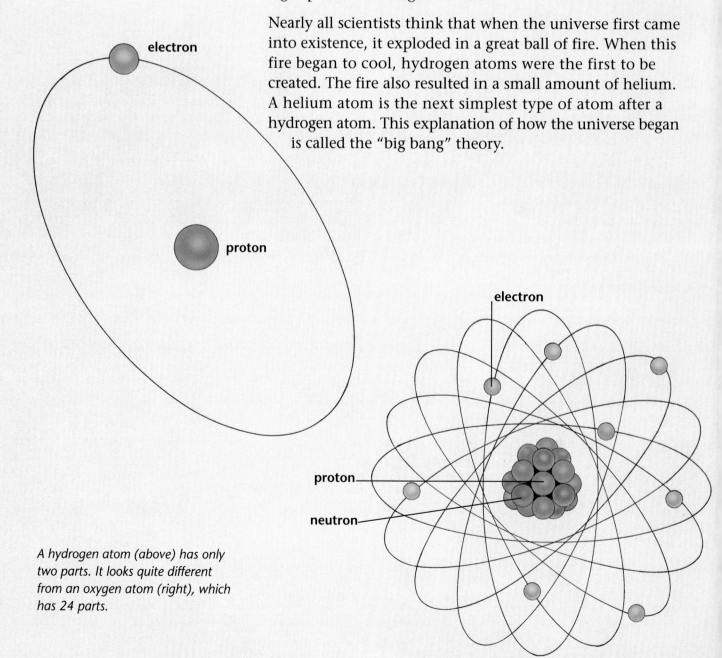

A hydrogen atom (above) has only two parts. It looks quite different from an oxygen atom (right), which has 24 parts.

Stars consist of hydrogen and helium gas. Hydrogen atoms are joining together, forming helium.

The first stars

Masses of hydrogen and helium atoms came together to form the first stars. Fusion inside other stars produced different and heavier types of atoms. This continued until the different kinds of matter in the universe had been created. This process is still going on now.

When we look at the sun and the stars, we are really looking at tremendous energy given off by hydrogen changing into helium. This process is known as **nuclear fusion.**

The universe is about 13 thousand million years old. After all this time, hydrogen and helium still make up nearly all the matter in space.

Gases and decay

One day, each plant and animal alive on Earth will die. If nothing happened to all these dead things, they would be left lying all over Earth. But that doesn't happen because when the cells of most living things die, they quickly start to change, or **decompose.**

Most of the decomposing work is done by tiny living things called **bacteria.** These break down the chemicals in dead plants and animals, and change them into simple substances. Some of these substances, such as nitrogen, return to the soil. Nitrogen helps produce new growth in plants. Fertilizers contain certain percentages of nitrogen, usually in combination with oxygen.

System for collecting gas

Modern landfills have been designed to control air pollution by controlling and collecting gases, such as methane, that are released by decomposing substances. Methane is used by chemical companies as a material to make other chemicals. Landfills also prevent water pollution by preventing decomposing substances from getting into underground water supplies.

System for collecting decomposed substances

Gases from garbage

Some of the substances produced by decomposition are given off as gases. These include carbon dioxide, hydrogen, nitrogen, and oxygen. Another gas produced by decomposing substances is **methane.** Methane is a flammable gas that can cause dangerous explosions. That is why in the United States, open dumps of rotting garbage are illegal.

Today, most household waste that cannot be recycled is placed in **sanitary landfills.** Waste is collected and brought to sanitary landfills, where it is packed down firmly by tractors and covered with earth. Landfills are lined with plastic or clay to prevent decomposing substances from getting into underground water supplies.

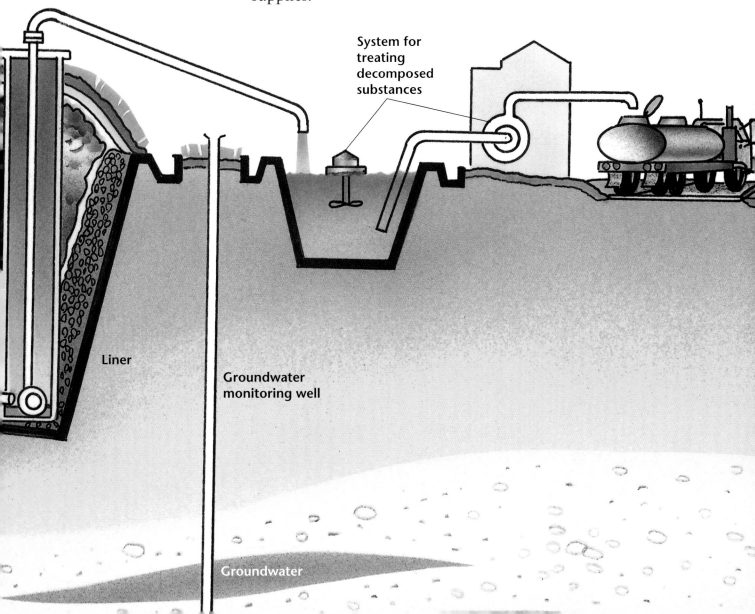

System for treating decomposed substances

Liner

Groundwater monitoring well

Groundwater

Find out more by looking
at pages   82–83
            86–87
           110–111
           114–115

Gases as fuels

Have you ever gone camping? If so, you might have used a portable gas cooking stove to prepare your food. This type of stove uses gas that has been put into a bottle under pressure. As you switch on the stove, the gas comes out through a nozzle. It can then be lit to provide heat for cooking. This type of gas is often called bottled gas. It is usually either butane or propane, or sometimes a mixture of both.

Producing gases from oil

Butane and propane differ from methane in one important way. Methane is found naturally beneath the earth's surface, but butane and propane are produced from oil.

Oil is a mixture of different substances that boil and condense at different temperatures. After the oil is pumped up from below the ground, it is split by heating processes into these different substances at a refinery.

Crude oil vapor passes into a huge distillation column. The different types of substances separate. The light gas rises to the top, and the heaviest oil sinks to the bottom.

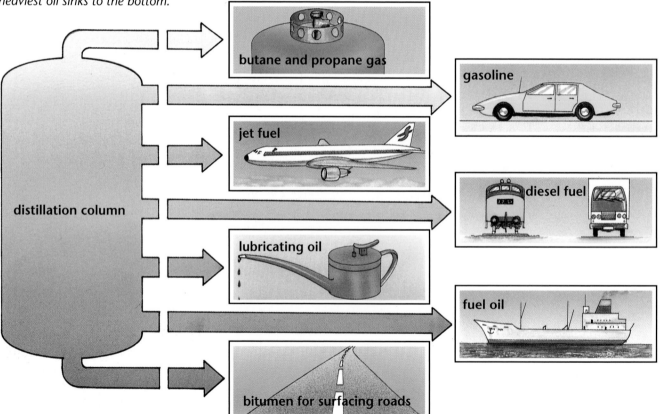

coal

air in   steam in

gases

The gases given off by burning coal are cleaned, or purified, as they pass through steam and water. Coal gas provides less heat than natural gas.

cooler

tar out

At the refinery

First, the oil is boiled in a furnace and the vapor mixture passes into the **distillation column.** As the vapors rise up the column, they cool and condense to form liquids. Butane and propane come out of the top as gases. They are condensed into liquids so that they can be easily transported to factories. The liquid gas is then bottled under pressure.

Gas from gasworks

Gas can also be produced by heating coal and then collecting the gases that escape. These include methane and hydrogen. **Coal gas,** also known as **coke oven gas,** is a by-product of the coke-making process. Today it is used mostly at the plants where it is produced.

At one time, coal gas was used in homes and other factories as well as at the coke-making plants. But there was one big problem with this type of gas. It was poisonous. Most gas supplied in towns and cities now is natural gas. It doesn't contain carbon monoxide and is less poisonous. **Natural gas** is an odorless mixture of gases found beneath the earth.

gases out

dust separator

fine ash and dust out

Find out more by looking at pages **110–111** **112–113**

Natural gas

The most important gas that we use as a source of energy is natural gas. We don't have to make this. It is found in deposits under the ground, usually near deposits of oil.

Natural gas is a mixture of several gases, including butane and propane. Most of it is methane. Natural gas comes from vegetation that decomposed millions of years ago.

Natural gas is used to provide heat for industry, and also for cooking and heating in our homes. It comes to our homes through pipes laid under the streets of towns and cities and across the countryside.

In some places, natural gas is piped directly from the gas production platforms, where it has been pumped up from beneath the seabed or from deep underground. In other places, it is shipped as a liquid in refrigerated tankers. It is pumped from the ships into storage tanks at the docks.

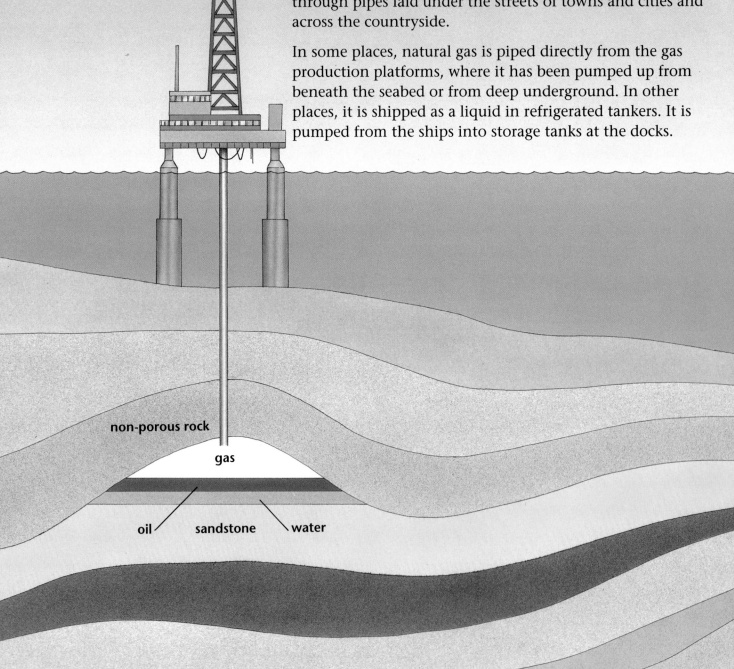

non-porous rock

gas

oil   sandstone   water

Natural gas is often found near deposits of oil. Gas production platforms pump the gas up from underground or from beneath the seabed.

Adding a smell

Unlike gas made in gasworks, natural gas doesn't have an odor. This means that we would not be able to tell if a pipe were leaking gas into the air. Because natural gas is mostly methane, it can easily explode when mixed with oxygen. So a smell is added to the gas before it reaches us to help us detect any possible leaks.

Supplies are limited

The world's supply of natural gas, formed millions of years ago, won't last forever. Scientists cannot agree about how long supplies will last, but it could be as little as 75 years. By then, methane might be available from sources such as sewage. When bacteria break down sewage at the sewage treatment plant, methane is given off. This gas could be collected and stored as a fuel.

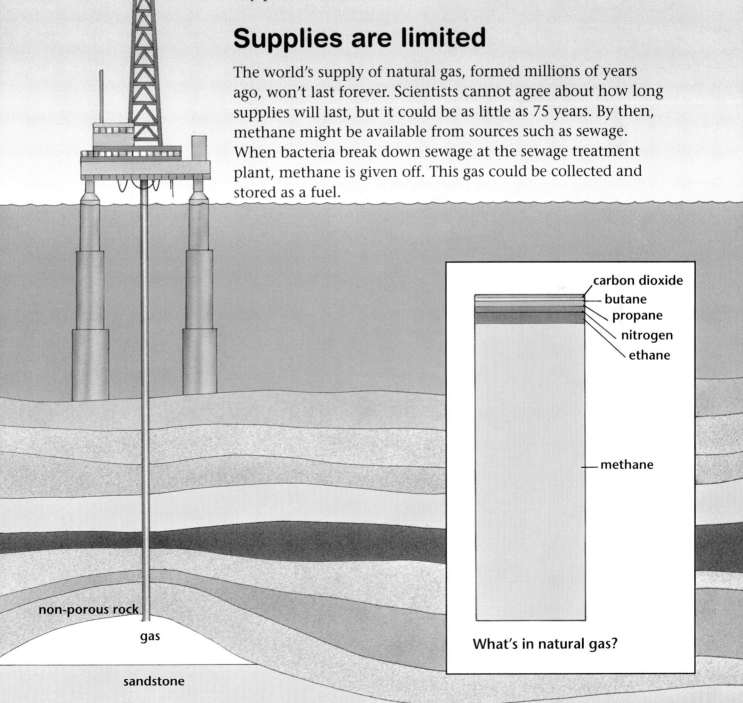

non-porous rock

gas

sandstone

carbon dioxide
butane
propane
nitrogen
ethane

methane

What's in natural gas?

Find out more by looking at pages **94–95**

Gases and light

Have you ever looked closely at an ordinary electric light bulb? Hold it carefully while you do so. Inside, you may see wire "legs" holding up a thinner wire arranged in a coil.

How does a light bulb work?

When a light bulb is switched on, electricity flows along the thin wire and makes it glow. Why does it glow white, and not red like the wire in an electric heater? Why doesn't the thin wire quickly burn out?

Many bulbs are filled mostly with **argon** gas. Because argon is **inert**, or chemically inactive, it allows the wire to glow brightly without burning. If the bulbs were filled with air or oxygen, the wire would be destroyed by burning. The wire glows white because it is so hot—over 4500 °F (2482 °C). And it doesn't melt because it's made of a metal called **tungsten**, which melts only at extremely high temperatures.

Many of the colors in the bright lights of Hong Kong come from different gases inside the light bulbs and tubes.

Halogen lamps help this airplane to land on the runway. This type of light can be seen even in daylight and in fog.

Gases in bulbs

Sometimes the gas inside a lamp produces a colored light. Different gases glow in different colors. Street lights that shine yellow contain sodium as a gas. Neon gas glows orange-red, and krypton makes a greenish-yellow light. In fact, different mixtures of gases in special lamps can produce many different colors.

In these lights, the electricity doesn't flow along a wire. It flows through the gas inside a thin, glass tube, making the gas glow. In a city at night, you can see lamps lighting up advertisements. These often flash on and off. Neon mixed with other gases gives them their different colors.

Halogen light is especially useful because it can be seen through fog. So it is often used in the warning lights at airports. Xenon is a gas that can be seen from long distances. That's why the high-powered electric lamps used in some lighthouses may contain xenon. Xenon is also used in the tubes of electronic flash units in cameras.

Air pressure: Pressure caused by the weight of the air.

Alloy: Metal formed when two or more metals are mixed together.

Atmosphere: Air surrounding Earth.

Atom: Smallest part of a substance. An atom contains a mass of *protons* and *neutrons* in a center called a *nucleus* that is surrounded by *electrons.* Everything is made of atoms.

Bacteria: Tiny living things that break down chemicals in dead plants and animals.

Boiling point: Temperature at which liquid bubbles and changes into gas.

Catalyst: Substance that produces a chemical reaction in other substances without itself changing.

Combustion: The process by which oxygen in the air combines with either a solid or another gas to give off energy. This energy is given off in the form of heat, and usually light, too.

Compound: Solid, liquid, or gas made up of a combination of atoms of more than one element.

Condensation: Process by which a gas changes into a liquid.

Conductor: Element that carries heat, electricity, or another form of energy.

Crystal: Tiny particle formed when liquids cool or solutions dry out. Crystals contain many angles and flat surfaces that repeat over and over.

Decompose: The process by which the cells of living things die and quickly start to change.

Density: Amount of matter in a unit volume of any substance.

Dissolve: To make a substance slowly break apart in another substance, usually a liquid.

Distillation: Process that separates a substance or a mixture of substances from a solution by boiling a liquid and condensing the vapor that forms.

Electrode: Point in a *solution* where an electric current enters and leaves the solution.

Electrolysis: Process by which electricity is passed through a substance.

Electron: Tiny particle that circles around the *nucleus* of an atom. It carries a negative electrical charge. The flow of many electrons is an electric current.

Electroplating: Method of making a metal coating by means of electricity.

Element: One of 109 identified basic materials from which everything in the universe is made.

Energy: The ability to do work.

Evaporation: Process by which a liquid or solid changes into a gas.

Freezing point: Temperature at which a liquid turns into a solid.

Fusion, nuclear: The combining of two atomic nuclei to create a nucleus of greater mass. This process gives stars their tremendous energy.

Gas: Substance that is not liquid or solid and has no shape or size of its own.

Humidity: Amount of water vapor contained in the air.

Hydrocarbon: Carbon and hydrogen atoms joined together. Hydrocarbons are very useful because they can be used to make many different substances.

Inert: Chemically inactive.

Inertia: The tendency of a motionless object to remain motionless, and of a moving object to continue moving at a constant speed and in the same direction. Inertia is a property of all *matter.*

Insoluble: Not able to *dissolve* in a liquid.

Kindling temperature: Lowest temperature at which an object begins to burn.

Liquid: Substance that flows freely from place to place.

Mass: The amount of *matter* in an object.

Matter: Anything that takes up space and has *inertia.*

Melting point: Temperature at which a solid turns into a liquid.

Metal: Substance that reflects light, has a shiny surface, is a good conductor of heat and electricity, and can be easily bent. Most elements are metals.

Methane: A flammable gas that is produced by decomposing substances.

Molecule: Smallest unit remaining when a substance has been divided as much as possible without having undergone a chemical change.

Natural gas: Gas used as a source of energy. It is found under the ground, usually near oil.

Neutron: Tiny particle found in the *nucleus* of an atom. The number of neutrons found in an atom may vary.

Nonmetal: Any element that does not share all the characteristics of a metal.

Nucleus: Central part of all atoms.

Ozone: Gas formed when ultraviolet rays from the sun change some of the oxygen in the *atmosphere.*

Pressure: Force pressing on something.

Property: Characteristic of a substance.

Proton: Tiny particle in the *nucleus* of an atom. It carries a positive electric charge.

Radioactive: Containing energy that is created by atoms breaking up.

Radiocarbon dating: Method of measuring the age of rocks and fossils, bones, and even ancient cloth by measuring the amount of *radioactive* material left in the substance.

Reaction, chemical: Chemical action of two substances that results in the formation of additional substances.

Sanitary landfill: A special area where household and other waste is buried and sealed off.

Smelting: Special heating method by which metals are taken from their original mineral or rock.

Solid: Substance that is not a liquid or gas.

Soluble: Able to *dissolve* in a liquid.

Solution: Mixture formed by *dissolving* one or more substances in a liquid.

Stratosphere: Layer of the *atmosphere* where ozone is found.

Superfluid: Liquid that doesn't follow the usual behavior of liquid.

Synthetic: Substance that is not natural, but has been made by people.

Thermosphere: The uppermost region of Earth's atmosphere.

Thrust: Force of high-pressure air.

Troposphere: Layer of the *atmosphere* where all the gases needed by living things on Earth are.

Vapor: Water boiled away as a gas.

Page numbers in *italic* type are references to illustrations.

Acknowledgements

The publishers of **World Book's** *Young Scientist* acknowledge the following photographers, publishers, agencies, and corporations for photographs used in this volume.

Cover	© PhotoDisc, Inc.
2–7	© PhotoDisc, Inc.
26/27	© Steven Kaufman, Bruce Coleman Collection
28/29	© E. Hummel, ZEFA Picture Library
30/31	© Brian Eyden, Science Photo Library
34/35	© Will and Deni McIntyre, Science Photo Library
40/41	© Spectrum Colour Library; © Maya Barnes, The Image Works
44/45	© ZEFA Picture Library
48/49	© Lawrie Brown
50/51	© ZEFA Picture Library
52/53	© Science Photo Library
54/55	© ZEFA Picture Library
56/57	© Paul Conklin, PhotoEdit
58/59	© H. Kraft, ZEFA Picture Library; © N. Bahnsen, ZEFA Picture Library
60/61	© Mark Richards, PhotoEdit
64–73	© Robert Harding Picture Library
74/75	© Robert Harding Picture Library; © ZEFA Picture Library
82/83	NASA from Science Photo Library
92/93	© Mike Hewitt, Allsport
94/95	© Spectrum Colour Library
96/97	NASA; © Larry Mitchell, Photo Researchers
104/105	© Robert Harding Picture Library
106/107	© Spectrum Colour Library
108/109	© ZEFA Picture Library
116/117	© KALT from ZEFA Picture Library; © DAMM from ZEFA Picture Library

Illustrated by

Martin Aitchinson
Nigel Alexander
Hemesh Alles
Martyn Andrews
Sue Barclay
Richard Berridge
John Booth
Lou Bory
Maggie Brand
Stephen Brayfield
Bristol Illustrators
Colin Brown
Estelle Carol
David Cook
Marie DeJohn
Richard Deverell
Farley, White and Veal
Sheila Galbraith
Peter Geissler
Jeremy Gower
Kathie Kelleher
Stuart Lafford

John Lobban
Louise Martin
Annabel Milne
Yoshi Miyake
Donald Moss
Eileen Mueller Neill
Teresa O'Brien
Paul Perreault
Roberta Polfus
Jeremy Pyke
Trevor Ridley
Barry Rowe
Don Simpson
Gary Slater
Lawrie Taylor
Gwen Tourret
Pat Tourret
Peter Visscher
David Webb
Gerald Whitcomb
Matthew White
Lynne Willey